Creating a Human Psychoanalytic Setting

This book looks at how psychoanalytic thinking can be applied in a variety of settings and can respect the individual experience and circumstances of each patient.

It focuses on the analytic encounter and the hard task around trying to create what the author calls a human analytic setting, one which respects human diversity and theoretical pluralism and pays adequate attention to the patient's emotional pain and suffering, while hopefully facilitating psychic change. Starting by looking at general features of independent psychoanalysis, the author explores institutional and political issues that can either facilitate or restrict psychoanalytic thinking and institutional life. He also explores key themes such as the nature of subjectivity, subject relations, and the nature of absence and presence, through case studies. The final chapters elaborate on the duality of the psychoanalyst's identity – one centred around the psychoanalyst's need for a home base for their confidence as practitioners and the other about the challenges facing analysts having to work in solitude for much of their working life.

With a focus on the intimate relationship between what happens in the analytic setting and the analyst's own institutional influences, this is key reading for psychoanalysts and psychotherapists.

Dr Roger Kennedy is a consultant child psychiatrist, adult psychoanalyst, and a past president of the British Psychoanalytical Society. He was an NHS consultant at the Cassel Hospital for 30 years and is now chair of the Child and Family Practice, where he sees children and families. He has had sixteen previous books published on psychoanalysis, interdisciplinary studies, and child work, as well as many papers.

Creating a Human Psychoanalytic Setting
Clinical Studies

Roger Kennedy

Routledge
Taylor & Francis Group

LONDON AND NEW YORK

Designed cover image: Getty Images

First published 2026
by Routledge
4 Park Square, Milton Park, Abingdon, Oxon OX14 4RN

and by Routledge
605 Third Avenue, New York, NY 10158

Routledge is an imprint of the Taylor & Francis Group, an informa business

For Product Safety Concerns and Information please contact our EU representative GPSR@taylorandfrancis.com. Taylor & Francis Verlag GmbH, Kaufingerstraße 24, 80331 München, Germany.

British Library Cataloguing-in-Publication Data
A catalogue record for this book is available from the British Library

ISBN: 9781041162001 (hbk)
ISBN: 9781041154402 (pbk)
ISBN: 9781003683315 (ebk)

DOI: 10.4324/9781003683315

Typeset in Optima
by codeMantra

Contents

Acknowledgements

- Chapters 2, 6, and 10 are adaptations of papers originally published in the *International Journal of Psychoanalysis*.
- An original version of Chapter 8 was published in my Routledge book *The Psychic Home* (2014).

1   Introduction
Creating a Human Analytic Setting

I will begin this book of clinical papers by looking at some general features of independent psychoanalysis, then at some of the institutional and political issues that can either facilitate or restrict psychoanalytic thinking and institutional life, and then move to the analytic encounter itself and the hard task around trying to create what I have called a human analytic setting, one that respects human diversity and theoretical pluralism, pays adequate attention to the patient's emotional pain and suffering, while hopefully facilitating psychic change. I will assume that there is an intimate relationship between what happens in the analytic setting and the analyst's own institutional influences, the latter affecting how the analyst listens to the patient and what interpretations are made.

With this approach in mind, subsequent chapters will tackle some of the other key themes that have preoccupied me over my career since I began psychoanalytic training in 1976, starting with a central preoccupation – the nature of subjectivity and the development of a psychoanalytic subject relations theory to complement object relations theory. I include a recent rethink of earlier thoughts about subject relations. This leads to some general points about the nature of absence and presence, through some light-hearted thoughts about the role of fathers, and later to clinical papers, two based upon case studies of challenging patients, an ill adolescent and a borderline man, and one focused on the nature of incest and its impact on psychic development. I include two papers concerning the psychoanalyst's identity – one centred around the psychoanalyst's need for a home base for their confidence as practitioners, the other about the challenges facing analysts having to work in solitude for much of their working life. Finally, I have included a few thoughts and aphorisms picked out from the journals I have kept from time to time, particularly focused on the writing of a book. I have called the chapter outtakes as I include material that generally did not get included in a book or a paper. That, of course, leaves out the many outtakes from actual sessions, the thoughts and comments coming from analyst and patient that never get recorded except somewhere in each partner's unconscious.

DOI: 10.4324/9781003683315-1

Independent Psychoanalysis

Though there is great interest in independent analysis abroad, with increasing attention paid to the thought of Winnicott, those in the United Kingdom who see his thought as a deep influence are very much in a minority, perhaps even an endangered species. I am not sure if we need special protection against our predators, or to be placed in a separate reserve where we can increase our numbers, though that at times feels like a temptation. But I certainly feel that we are at a crossroads and need to have a view about which path to take before it is too late.

Psychoanalysts, of course, cannot put aside the particular and potentially fateful, or fatal, resonances that come with the notion of a crossroads, given the importance in analytic theory of the Oedipus story, and his murderous encounter with his father Laius at the place where *three paths* met. I have always wondered what those three paths were, apart from any symbolism, such as representing past, present, and future. One path led back to where Oedipus came from and yet was not his original home, Corinth; another led to Thebes, where he became King, which was where he was born but from which he was expelled as a baby; but where did that enigmatic other path lead to? Or was it there to remind us that there is always some other path we never do take, or we need to be there as another path?

But in general, a crossroads is a place where multiple paths meet. Some time ago, I made the point that there are many ways of practicing and understanding psychoanalysis, both as a clinical treatment and in its interaction with other disciplines. That is, there are what I called *many voices* in the analytic field, each of them bringing something potentially valuable. Each analyst then must find a particular kind of approach that more congenially matches their own quality of listening, development, character, values, prejudices, and ambitions. One must find one's own analytic voice or identity; this is a constant process, involving coming to grips with what the American critic Harold Bloom[1] called the 'anxiety of influence.'

Freud's influence is still profound, even if we are surrounded by various kinds of influence-anxiety. Freud's thought continues to be transmitted in a variety of ways – through his texts, through different psychoanalytic schools, and from analyst to patient. The reading and re-reading of Freudian texts requires that we both go back to Freud but also read Freud as a contemporary, connecting his text with the living practice of the present. This is a hermeneutic activity up to a point; where it diverges from hermeneutics is that psychoanalysis is primarily an oral, clinical activity, a technique or craft. We should not have pupils in analysis; even in training analyses, for that is potentially dangerous, leading to indoctrination, where the analyst's voice takes precedence over the candidate's voice.

However, around the analytic experience there is teaching of theory and technique, out of which arise, as in any other body of knowledge, issues of mastery, influence, rivalry, transmission of tradition, betrayals, subversions, power relations, as well as the positive influence of apprenticeship, where mutual exchange and learning of skills and craft can take place.

Finding one's own voice then is a complex process, involving some kind of nuanced discipleship, where managing multiple influences has to be worked through in some way.

Relevant to these issues is a quote from Freud's brief yet powerfully evocative paper on Family Romances[2]: [my own translation.]

> The freeing up of the individual, as he grows up, from the authority of his parents is one of the most necessary but also most painful achievements of development. It is absolutely necessary that this should occur, and it may be presumed that it has been to some extent achieved by everyone who has reached a normal state. Indeed, the progress of society is based upon the opposition between successive generations.

Having outlined what happens in normal development, Freud then turns to neurotics, some of whom have failed in this task. The family romance is the name for fantasies where the subject imagines that his relationship to his parents has been modified, so that for example he might fantasize that he is an adopted child or has noble parents. Rather than face the conflicting Oedipal feelings towards one or both parents, the child creates a fantasy of being special or of having other, however idealized, parents.

Thus, Freud's paper seems to imply that progress in (Western) society depends upon the opposition between generations, that discipleship of necessity requires rejection, and that it is only neurotics who cannot face this opposition and hence avoid liberation.

One might ask, then, are we the true-born children of our analytic parents? Can we only become free by opposition? Hopefully not. If psychoanalysis continues on this oppositional path, scorning those who do not follow the 'one true path,' demanding allegiance rather than respectful recognition of different viewpoints and approaches, I cannot see much of a future for it in an increasingly pluralistic world.

I have summarized some of the typical features of the pluralistic independent analytic approach before.[3] These are, in brief, a certain kind of receptivity to what the patient says, a trust in the unconscious, bearing states of unknowing and openness to the unknown, while also being aware of the realities of the external environment and how they impact on the patient's life. Technique is important, but it needs to be flexible and responsive, and not from 'on high.' The analyst is not all-knowing, giving constant transference interpretations because they know what is going on and want to 'show' the patient what they are doing. Reconstruction of history is vital, as is a flexible attitude to analytic theory; whatever works may be of some use, provided it aids the patient's associations and the analytic process. A collaborative or intersubjective approach is common, and so is an awareness of the potentially traumatic nature of being in analysis; it is tough, and the patient may well need some ego support while going through the inevitable regressions involved in a successful analysis.

I will give just one clinical example from a past analysis to highlight the vital role of a patient's history in resolving unconscious conflicts and trauma, very much an Independent theme.

This involves a man in his 40s nearing the end of a long analysis. He had come into analysis because of a sense of emptiness and futility in personal and work relationships, as well as periods of depression. He had a traumatic early history, in that his mentally ill mother was subject to repeated hospital admissions for quite florid psychotic behaviour. His father, a more stable but somewhat emotionally distant figure, spent periods away from the family home on various kinds of business. My patient, in fact, found some stability in attending a male boarding school, together with his younger brother, to whom he was not that close, but learned there to hide his emotions and to turn to academic achievement as a way of finding some self-regard. Despite these early difficulties, he had managed to marry and have a successful career, a marriage, and children, but was always haunted by the ill mother.

The period of ending the analysis was, not surprisingly, emotionally difficult, yet also productive, as can be seen in this excerpt from a session a few months before the end.

He was worried about how he got into entangled relationships, muddled up and confused. He described some situations at work when he felt he was being drawn into behaving like a rival for his mother's attention and linked this to his feelings about his younger brother, whom he felt was favoured by his mother. His mother had, in fact, had her first major psychotic breakdown after my patient's birth, and the theme of feeling responsible for her illness had been a major element of the analysis.

My patient then said that what he had got from the analysis was a way of fighting through all these problems, without losing the thread anymore. But he was fearful about how he was going to do this without coming to see me. I linked this fear to one we had frequently talked about before, about how to separate from a mentally ill mother. He replied by suddenly remembering a fragment of a *dream*. This was that he had pain in the soles of his feet.

He said that this was a bit weird and wondered what it meant. Something about pain, he added. I replied that maybe it was something about another kind of 'soul,' and about a painful soul, how he was going to deal with that kind of pain. This led to him thinking about how he dealt with emotional pain, tending in the past to distance himself, although now he was more able to face conflicts, as he had described at his work. He said he needed to find a *space to feel pain* 'without disintegration and madness.' He was thinking about the next phase of his life. He mentioned a book he was reading about a brother and sister who were 'fused' with one another. That led to more thoughts about him and his mother, what he had had to deal with, with her bizarre behaviour, how he had to defend himself against her intrusion, and also his fear of being 'fused' with her. However, he did feel that he could lead a life of his own. He could now feel he could be happy with his family, but he was also afraid of how the ending was going to be, what kind of life he was going to live. He ended the session by wondering what the next phase of his life was going to be.

While, of course, there was considerably more work to be done around the ending of the analysis, the patient was much more able to deal with conflicting emotions. As he put it, he now had a way of fighting through his problems without losing the thread, or one might say without being taken over by his mother's illness. As so often the case with such patients, one of the main tasks of the analysis is to sort out how much a patient is muddled up with the parent's psychosis, which becomes an alien presence as it were. This work concerns separating the patient's own disturbance from that of their parent's disturbance, or of trying to diminish the unhappiness that gets passed down the generations. The patient was able to have more lasting periods of happiness with his family because as he put it he had begun to find a space to experience emotional pain and to manage almost unbearable trauma. Then this piece of work, of course, became part of the history of the analysis and therefore a piece of the patient's new reality.

In Defence of Pluralism

I think that Independent analysis is consistent with Hannah Arendt's view that one should remain suspicious of the existence of a single compelling truth (though not evidenced facts), and that instead one should rejoice in the unending discourse among people in search of the truth but never reaching a single source of truth; the notion of a single truth only leads to inhumanity.

Arendt[4] describes this *pluralistic thinking* as a special form of *tolerance*, involving the gift of friendship, openness to the world and with the genuine love of mankind. The ideal of absolute truth, that she describes in its extreme form in *totalitarian* regimes, threatens in all societies the political public space between people, which she prioritizes as the site of freedom, a space in which there is room to consider different perspectives and reach sound political judgments and room to stand back from one's immediate feelings and loyalties and strive for impartiality.

If men united in a single opinion, she states,

> so that out of many opinions one would emerge, as though not men in their infinite plurality but man in the singular, one species and its exemplars, were to inhabit the earth…the world, which can only form in the interspaces between men in all their variety, would vanish altogether.[5]

Arendt argues that pluralism is essential to preserve humanity. She gives us a powerful vision of a *tolerant public space*, which, while open to all, needs to guard against the forces of intolerance, those who limit open and public discourse, often in the name of some single and abiding 'truth.'

Pluralism does not imply confusion, or lack of coherence or wooliness, something which Independent analysts have been accused of in the past and even now and have perhaps not done enough to counter. It requires considerable and hard-won discipline, in the process of focusing down on what makes sense for a particular situation. This does not imply a lack of focus or an 'anything goes' approach, but a disciplined, open-minded yet flexible approach to responding to what the patient brings. As Eric Rayner[6] put it,

> Commitment to open-mindedness in any endeavour requires self-discipline of a high order when complex issues are being evaluated. This is certainly the case in analysis. It should also be added...that the Independents' empirical ethic gives no encouragement to that quality of cruelty which can emerge in the minds of strict adherents to a doctrine after it has started to become sterile.

I think that such strict adherence to one way of working and thinking is a reaction to the uncomfortable fact that much of what we do is pretty messy and uncertain, like most things of importance in life. Donald Schön has put this rather well in his book The Reflective Practitioner:

> In the varied topography of professional practice, there is the high, hard ground where practitioners can make effective use of research-based theory and technique, and there is the swampy lowland where situations are confusing "messes" incapable of technical solution. The difficulty is that the problems of the high ground, however great their technical interest, are often relatively unimportant to clients or to the larger society, while in the swamp are the problems of greatest human concern.[7]

Descending to the messy swamp of pluralism means engaging with the most important and challenging problems, where trial and error, intuition and muddling through are the order of the day. This often means judging what to do by the 'feel' of things.

Pluralism is also very much a contemporary theme in other disciplines and reflects the global world we live in. Just to give one example, that of music. After the second world war, there was a reaction against old musical languages, and an explosion of new, very modern musical languages intent on creating music divorced entirely from the sort of mystical self-expression and nationalism that were perceived as being responsible for fascism and Nazism. Serialism, pushed forward for example by Pierre Boulez, involved the denial of tonality and even the expression of beauty in music, the latter seen as a reflection of an old and outmoded world that had led to the catastrophes of the second world war. Pre-existing structures, such as the triad, the basis of tonality, were eliminated. I think one can see similar developments at that time even in psychoanalysis, with a search at that time in the 50s for unitary thinking aimed at inclusive explanations, such as in the work of Klein and Lacan.

However, in music, as in many other fields today, pluralism has become acceptable and desirable. Pluralism in music describes a compositional philosophy: the willingness, for expressive reasons, to employ a range of different musical languages within a single piece and even within a single movement. Heightened music expression and even beauty have returned to the concert hall – much to the relief of the audiences. The serialists had forgotten the way that music is actually perceived by the listener.

In my own work, I have looked at what drives people to become intolerant towards pluralism. In my book on tolerance and intolerance[8] I made the point that they inevitably go together; there is a dynamic between them. I also suggested that what often drives intolerance of others and other opinions and views is a fear of losing one's identity. I described in this book and the previous one[9] how a fear of a loss of home, or more fundamentally a fear of a loss of a psychic structure which provides a central core of our identity a – *psychic home* – accounts for a considerable amount of prejudiced and intolerant attitudes to strangers, as well as towards anyone who has different ways of being and thinking.

One can often see this dynamic in psychoanalytic institutions, who fiercely hold onto particular ways of reacting, or beliefs about their ways of working. This becomes like a psychic home, a hard-won base as it were. Inevitably then intolerance of other ways of working gets set up, as if the hard-won psychic home is under threat. The point is that this sort of dynamic is inevitable. 'We have our psychic home; we don't want them over there spoiling it. Let's put up a wall against them.'

To move beyond unconsciously acting out this dynamic to addressing intolerant attitudes and changing them requires considerable work. To achieve what I have called *subject tolerance*, where there is respect for the other and others as subjects *of* their experience, with agency and capacity for independent judgment, requires a *tolerant imaginative internal space* in people's minds. This contrasts with '*object tolerance*,' where the other and others are seen as mere objects, to be put up with or confined in a walled area, or ghetto, or behind a barrier of indifference or hatred.

I cannot see how such institutional issues about the need for an open public space for discussion cannot impact on what happens between an analyst and patient in the consulting room, where a more intimate and private space needs to be created. Without the backing of a tolerant institutional space, it can be very difficult managing to preserve plural ways of thinking and working.

A Human Analytic Setting

I would suggest that a pluralistic approach to psychoanalytic thinking of necessity is intimately linked to what I have called a human analytic setting, one where there is respect for the complexities of the patient's inner world, and which, starting specifically from what the patient says, allows the patient's many voices to be heard and is not closed down by too rigid, or even cruel, attitudes from the analyst. As it is the union of the patient's words with the analyst's close listening to what has been said which then leads to interpretation, facilitating a human analytic setting involves particular attitudes to *listening* and *interpretation*, which I will examine in turn.

Listening

In my view a human analytic setting involves a kind of *pluralistic or fluid way of listening* to the patient. How one listens usually varies as the analysis progresses. There are no rigid rules about how an analysis progresses, but one can often trace what Serge Viderman[10] described as three basic phases. Occasionally the phases merge quickly into one; but mostly a *process* develops.

In the early or *pre-transference stage*, I usually take time to get to know the patient and their story. It may take time before unconscious themes begin to cohere. Listening and waiting are important, so as not to close off the associations. Of course, if a patient is highly anxious, one may need to quickly address their surface anxieties. This is a matter of what Ferenczi[11] called 'tact,' or basic empathy, which will protect us from unnecessarily stimulating the patient's resistance, or doing so at the wrong moment.

There is then often the emergence of *scattered transference reactions*. We are in the presence of true transference manifestations, but they are still relatively amorphous, not yet cohering into a stable picture. The patient may want an ordinary social relationship at this point. Listening then gradually leads to interventions enabling the transference to deepen. For me that means trying to hear the patient's deep unconscious themes, with only occasional comments and the occasional interpretation.

The phase of the *transference proper* feels as if one is immersed in a more freely associating environment; there is an analytic process. There is a closer relationship between listening and interpretation. The listening then becomes more like evenly suspended attention, as the patient is probably at this point just getting on with being in analysis.

It is then that one may be able to make sense of how the patient listens to what the analyst says. How the patient listens to the analyst's interpretation can lead to the analyst then finding new meaning to what was said, après-coup, or what Haydeé Faimberg[12] calls 'listening to listening.'

Psychoanalysis is a listening discipline; its bedrock is listening deeply to the patient. While of course there are significant differences between listening to a musical performance and listening to a patient in a consulting room, there is also some common ground. In psychoanalytical listening, one is listening simultaneously to the 'surface' and the 'depth' of the patient's communications, to both the conscious and underlying unconscious stream of thoughts and feelings. There are some loose parallels with this kind of listening and musical analysis, particularly the kind that looks beneath the surface of the musical 'foreground' to the underlying deep structures of the 'background.' However, such analysis is a highly sophisticated and intellectual exercise.

Analytic listening, in contrast, however intellectually taxing at times, also entails a responsive, receptive or affective kind of listening, more like trying to make sense of the shape of the communications or their vitality affects, the dynamic quality of the emotions. This has also been described as a kind of musical 'reverie,'[13] which can arise in the analyst particularly during intense emotional exchanges. Theodor Reik, who saw music as intimately linked to emotions and psychic reality, had already pointed out, with many clinical examples, how musical associations arising in the analyst's mind can be of great help in the understanding of the patient's communications.

> The tunes occurring to the analyst during sessions with patients are preconscious messages of thoughts that are not only meaningful, but also important for the understanding of the emotional situation of the patient…The tunes stand in the service of the agents responsible for the communication between the unconscious of two persons.[14]

Just to give one simple example given by Reik: A patient has a dream. *She is in the bath and is worried because she has forgotten to take off her watch which could be ruined if it gets wet.* There were no helpful associations to the dream. In the pause between her report of the dream and the following sentences she spoke, a long-forgotten tune came to Reik's mind, which he then realized he had not heard since childhood. The title was *The Watch* (by Karl Löwe). He recalled later the first lines: 'Wherever I go, I carry a watch with me always, and only need to look whenever I'd know the time of day.' The watch meant the human heart. Reik then recalled the phrase that Viennese girls used to say, referring to their periods, that 'with me it is punctual as a watch.' At the next session, the patient referred to her dream and said that she had forgotten to put in her diaphragm after her bath, and was worried that intercourse might have led to a pregnancy.

One could say that every patient has their own music, but that every analyst and patient encounter creates a music of its own. The analyst is thus engaged with listening to both the patient and to themselves and to their own responses to what the patient brings. Thus, as Michael Parsons has shown,[15] analysis involves listening in two dimensions at once – externally to their patients and internally to what is stirred up by listening to their patients. That internal listening involves a certain kind of receptivity to the unconscious, which seems to have parallels with listening to music. Being receptive to the 'internal' music aroused in a listening analyst helps the analyst understand the external music that is the patient.

During a session, the analyst may become immersed in the flow of the patient's material. As Martin Nass describes, 'As in listening to music, one may follow the melody line, the obbligato, the counterpoint. The analyst is free to move from one line to the other, to hear them all simultaneously.'[16]

The quality of communication between analyst and patient is similar to that of musicians in small ensembles; there is then a close mutual adjustment and readjustment of interaction, or *entrainment*, that is, the 'alignment or integration of bodily features with some recurrent features in the environment.'[17] Musical entrainment involves perceiving the regularity of beat and can be seen for example when dancing to music or marching in time to music. It seems hard-wired into the brain, since it is a skill that children can be seen to acquire naturally. There is even evidence that participating in musical activity such as synchronized singing and drumming can promote cooperation in four-year-olds.[18]

With musicians there is obviously a complex form of entrainment. This involves conscious and unconscious communications between the players, communication at both the bodily and emotional level, with the reading of gesture and eyes as well as the building up of trust and mutual understanding. Emotional focus, where the performers are enabled to be absorbed and focused *within* the music somehow seems to be a vital part of giving a good performance and requires this sort of close common understanding and communication.

Perhaps we can understand some aspects of the psychoanalytic relationship in these terms, where there may be different degrees of entrainment between analyst and patient, depending upon the nature of what gets repeated in the transference.

I don't think we emphasize enough that the analytic encounter takes place within a complex boundaried *sound world* or *soundscape*, in which hearing takes precedence over seeing. Freud's use of the couch was a radical way of pushing the sound world to the fore in treatment. The distribution in space of things heard is fundamentally different from that of things seen.[19] Sight tends to distance us from things; there is a landscape which we can admire but it remains out there. Figures may move in a landscape but the landscape we see does not move. But hearing envelops us. 'Sound, by its enveloping character, brings us closer to everything alive.'[20]

To see without hearing is to witness an uncanny dumb show and is disorienting. But to hear without seeing, as in closing one's eyes, can be revelatory. One gets more profoundly in touch with moods, emotions, and the meaning of words.

'Hearing *musical* sound, with or without words, makes us especially aware of proximity and thus connectedness. Parents sing lullabies to their infants, and their infants respond: this is music at its most enveloping.'[21]

Because music occurs in time, it can under certain circumstances provide a powerful sense of *continuity,* basic to the soundscape and to many features of the analytic setting. Already with the early mother-baby relationship, one can see how the maternal voice echoes and re-echoes to the baby's sounds, in a kind of musical manner, imitating and repeating what comes from the baby and providing, as Daniel Anzieu[22] describes, as a sort of sound mirror, not a static mirror but a dynamic and responsive mirror providing a sense of continuity over time. In distorted mother-baby relationships, for example, with a depressed or borderline mother, there may be a lack of responsiveness, and the maternal echo can become more like the plaintive echo in the myth of narcissus, and time can become deadly, what Green has called 'dead time.'[23] Anzieu also describes how the sound mirror can become pathogenic when the mother's response is dissonant, contradicting what the baby feels or expects; or can be too abrupt, causing confusion and psychic damage to the baby's protective defences; or impersonal, when the mirror of sounds fails to provide emotional information for the baby. Otherwise, the mother's vocal responses normally provide a positive experience for the baby, enveloping or wrapping the baby in a comforting and enlivening sound world.

Trevarthen and Gratier propose that the expressive rhythm of human voices, or the *communicative musicality* of the mother-baby interchange, has a vital role in promoting the well-being and comfort of the baby. Using Winnicott's notion of physical and mental holding, they propose that, 'the vocal rhythms of interpersonal engagement constitute a Holding environment for the infant that is in continuity and coherent with the physical holding involved in the caregiver's mothering techniques.'[24]

Studies of interactions between infants and problematic mothers confirm the crucial role of *voice*. Thus, mothers with postnatal depression speak to their babies with monotonous, low-pitched voices and have difficulty engaging in lively protoconversations or 'motherese.' Depressed mother's speech is less musically expressive and less focused on the infant.[25] Borderline mothers tend to be unpredictably intrusive or withdrawn and express more negative affect; their vocal performance is also inconsistent and dissonant, reflecting their shifting mood states, and that is confusing for the baby. Thus overall, one can say that communicative musicality is a vital element of bonding and attuned attachment between mother and infant. Without musicality the internalization from the interaction between voices is distorted and emotions are disturbed.

Daniel Stern[26] had described the important role of *vitality affects* in the mother-baby relationship. This was a way of trying to describe the dynamic quality of the emotions between mother and child, and how a mother may be 'tuned' into the baby's state of mind or on the contrary have difficulties in so doing. Affect attunement is an important quality in good enough mother child relationships, and something that needs to be looked at when considering the nature of attachments. He cited the work of Suzanne Langer[27] who had already paid attention to the many 'forms of feeling' inextricably involved with all the vital life processes. She had also used the notion of forms of feeling to capture the many feelings evoked by music. For her music does not so much evoke particular feelings but their 'form,' their essential shape over time.

In his later work, Stern[28] extended the notion of vitality affect and, rather in the manner of Langer, described the role of 'dynamic forms of vitality,' a mental creation shaping human experience, including the musical experience. Vitality forms can be described in terms of movement, time, force, space, and direction, all together giving the experience of vitality. Dynamic forms of vitality give life and shape to the narratives we create about our lives. We tend to think of the mother-baby interaction in terms of objects and space; the advantage of this way of thinking is that one is dealing with the 'real time' phenomena of process, dynamics and flow.

Nass also points out how new analytic themes in the analysis may arise and develop, repeat, and transform in ways similar to how they do so in a musical composition.

But if the analyst listens out for patterns, they may often be strange patterns. Some are coherent patterns, but more often than not we listen for breaks in the continuity, where the pattern is dissonant. That is where the conflicts may reside as it were.

Interpretation

A lot of passion seems to be spent in asserting that there is a 'right' way of giving interpretations to the patient. I don't think that's the best way to start thinking about interpretations. From my experience of listening to many sorts of trainees in supervision and seminars, I would say that there is something that one could call a 'convincing' interpretation, or way of interpreting. What makes it convincing depends upon the details of how the analyst listens in the session, the actual words they use when they talk with the patient and the timing of interventions, how emotionally in touch they are with the patient and their anxieties, and I would add the quality of understanding of the patient's present and past life and environment, including grasping any particularly significant or traumatic events. As you can no doubt appreciate, I think it is bizarre to forget the patient's past and only focus on the here and now. I think it is very important *not* to keep interpreting the whole time in order to facilitate the patient's associations. Too much insistence on making interpretations just closes off the unconscious. As Ferenczi put it,

> Above all, one must be sparing with interpretations, for one of the most important rules of analysis is to do no unnecessary talking; over-keenness in making interpretations is one of the infantile diseases of the analyst. When the patient's resistances have been analytically resolved, stages in the analysis are reached every now and then in which the patient does the work of interpretation practically unaided, or with only slight prompting from the analyst.[29]

That is, the analyst needs to have the capacity not to interpret and to know when not to, hopefully *opening up* unconscious communication rather than *closing it off*; aiming for *open* rather than *closed* interpretations.

Elsewhere,[30] I have suggested there were at least three reasons why analysts make interpretations. The first need is intellectual, the need to make sense of what is happening in the analysis, or, by interpreting, give or discover meaning. The second reason is an emotional one, that of wishing to make contact with the patient, and the third need was as a defence against the impact of the patient on the analyst as a result of being constantly in contact with powerful primitive processes.

One should add that the nature of the patient's associations varies considerably. Associations can be compulsive, apparently leading nowhere, defensive, or somehow free and more spontaneous, depending perhaps on how directly the patient is communicating with their unconscious.

It is, as I say, difficult to define what makes the handling of a session sound convincing, but maybe it's something about the quality of 'entrainment,' to go back to musical language, a kind of attuned interaction, though not necessarily an easy one.

Freud in his papers on technique makes the crucial point in the handling of dream interpretation, but also interpretation in general, that the appropriate analytic stance is to give up conscious purposive aims and be *guided by the unconscious* in establishing links.[31]

Analysts vary greatly on the interpretation of what Freud means here. I also think that analysts vary greatly in how they can read unconscious communications in their patients and in themselves. Experience of doing many years of analysis does help, particularly experience of undertaking intensive analysis rather than less intense psychotherapy.

The French style of psychoanalysis is very much towards interpretations which directly pick up and name unconscious themes, though for example a verbal allusion, a play of irony, or just a judicious comment.

For example, Serge Viderman[32] reported a patient's dream: 'My father and I are in a garden. I pick some flowers and offer him a bouquet of six roses.' He said to his patient, wanting to illuminate the *thorns* hidden in the gift of roses, 'Six roses or cirrhose.' (Cirrhosis). The patient's father had in fact died as a result of alcoholic excess.

Slips of the tongue, witticisms, and puns are of course nearer to the unconscious. Symptoms themselves can play sorts of language games with the body. A judicious use of verbal play is a form of interpretation. I certainly would use this occasionally as a way of making a point, or of trying to help the patient get in touch with their own unconscious life, or just to see what might happen. It can also sometimes make light of a very difficult situation and help the patient to face difficult issues from a different and less challenging perspective. An example of this form of exchange as one element of an interpretative exchange was when I linked sole to soul in the first clinical example.

In a psychoanalytic session, what will happen is, hopefully, uncertain. The analyst waits to see what will *emerge* in the patient's narrative, whether it be a dream, some unexpected thoughts, a series of free associations, fantasies, or surprising actions. This is what I would call waiting for those moments of *emerging subjectivity*. One can see this in the last example, when the patient is confronted with the dawning of the awareness of their own sibling rivalry, which they will need to own, rather than run away by ending the analysis.

From time to time, the analyst may be able to nudge the patient where appropriate and in the interests of the treatment, offering some kind of 'punctuation' of the narrative, either through comments or more organized transference interpretations. (I try to do both). The hope is that eventually, however long it takes, and of course it usually does take a long time, the patient will find their own voice. They will move from what I have called being subject 'to' their history to being subject 'of' their history, that is, more active agents.

The analytic setting provides a structure, a setting in which the indefinable can become definable, what one could call a *home for the unconscious*.

But for free association to happen, the analytic setting needs to be welcoming. Not free from conflict, not always comfortable of course, but welcoming the unconscious. This is what I mean by a human space.

Clearly analysts differ in what they hope will emerge in the analytic setting. I have described in Chapter 2 how one important way of describing *change* in analysis is through a process whereby the patient 'becomes a subject.' What I mean by this is as follows:

The patient brings all sorts of different stories, fixed patterns of relating or symptoms, hopes, expectations, and resistances. Patients often come with a sense of isolation; of either being alone with suffering or suffering from being alone. And they come to analysis subject to various forces in their life, past and present. If the analysis works, there is the possibility of their becoming *subject of* their experiences and ultimately of their lives, with a sense of being no longer isolated and more in contact with others. Becoming a subject, then, involves a shift towards a subjective position, where the subject has more capacity to take up different positions without their becoming fixed in a kind of frozen state of being. However, this shift can be both precarious and difficult to see or to define. One usually only has brief moments of illumination.

These precious moments may be most intense at various *crossroads* between the processes of coming and going, presence and absence, the past and the present, life and death; along paths taken and glimpses of paths not taken.

I have suggested that part of the analytic enterprise consists of a particular form of *listening and waiting* – for the emergence of something that is alive in the human subject. If our psychoanalytic work has any future, the message must surely be that our primary concern is with helping our patients find what is alive in themselves in a world that continues to find that difficult to hear and to bear.

Notes

1 Bloom (1997).
2 Freud (1909, p. 237).
3 Kennedy (2007).
4 Arendt (1970).
5 Arendt (1970, p. 31).
6 Rayner (1991, p. 205).

7 Schön (1983, p. 42).
8 Kennedy (2019).
9 Kennedy (2014).
10 Viderman (1979, p. 274).
11 Ferenczi (1928, p. 257).
12 Faimberg (2005).
13 Lombardi (2008).
14 Reik (1953, pp. 19–20).
15 Parsons (2014, p. 113ff).
16 Nass (1971, p. 309).
17 De Nora (2000, pp. 78–9).
18 Kirschner and Tomasello (2010, pp. 354–364).
19 Kramer (2018, pp. 86–87).
20 Leppert (1993, p. 29).
21 Leppert (1993, p. 29).
22 Anzieu (1995, p. 174).
23 Green (2003, p. 115).
24 Gratier and Trevarthen (2007, p. 174).
25 Murray et al. (1993, pp. 1083–1101).
26 Stern (1985, p. 54ff).
27 Langer (1967).
28 Stern (2010).
29 Ferenczi (1928).
30 Kennedy (2007, pp. 53–54).
31 Freud (1911, p. 94).
32 Viderman (1979, p. 264).

2 Becoming a Subject
Some Theoretical and Clinical Issues

I shall present a cluster of theoretical and clinical thoughts, and some clinical material concerned with the complex issue of subjectivity in psychoanalysis. For convenience, I have organized these thoughts around the notion of 'becoming a subject,' as this conveys to me something essential about what we are trying to do in the analytic encounter with adults. While the main aim is to present clinically relevant issues, I would suggest that the complexity of the issues involved in tackling subjectivity requires some preliminary theoretical considerations. A number of contemporary psychoanalytic thinkers are currently wrestling with the kinds of issues raised in this chapter and have very much influenced my own thinking in this area. Although there is considerable overlap with object relations theory, it does seem that what is currently taking place is pushing psychoanalysis into new territory, so much so that one could agree with Ogden that the analytic conception of the subject is the 'cornerstone of the psychoanalytic project,'[1] even though he added, at that time, that it was also the least well-articulated of psychoanalytic concepts. Hoffman[2] had already argued that we were witnessing the evolution of a new paradigm for understanding the psychoanalytic situation, which marked the beginnings of a new emphasis on subjectivity in psychoanalysis. Influenced by the work of Berger and Luckmann[3] on the sociology of knowledge, he called it the 'social-constructivist' paradigm. Berger and Luckmann emphasized how reality is socially constructed. It is neither already given nor created by individual endeavours alone but arises out of constant interaction between subjects. This social reality can be looked at as both an independent objective reality created by interaction and a subjective reality because society is built up by activity that expresses subjective meaning. Hoffman took account of the analyst's constant participation in the analytic process, which is created out of the interaction of analyst and patient; how there is a need to take account of the mutual influence of analyst and patient, and how meaning is constructed out of the analytic situation. I will refer to various analytic thinkers who are currently struggling with these sorts of issues, as well as some philosophical ideas that may help to clarify some of the complexities of this field, in the hope that something fruitful will arise out of this interaction with these other contributions.

DOI: 10.4324/9781003683315-2

First, one can ask what the term *subject* means in this context. It is a term that has many resonances, comprising a mixture of conscious and unconscious elements. For example, it refers to the conscious or unconscious subject of discourse, the one who speaks, the subject of a story or narrative; and it can imply a relationship to an object. It seems to include the idea of agency, being the subject of actions, and, as Benjamin[4] has described that of authorship, 'the condition of ownership that reflects intentionality and bestows awareness of others' states, feelings, and intentions.'[5] The term has both philosophical and political resonances. In one line of philosophical thinking, still dominant in much academic philosophy in Britain and North America, the subject refers to the conscious, thinking subject, the subject of conscious reason. While the political subject is a citizen with certain fundamental rights, such as that of belonging to civil society and having the right to vote, the term implies being subject to a higher authority. The Freudian subject, a unique construct, incorporates ambiguity, uncertainty, and paradox, which follows from the existence of an unconscious. At the heart of our subjectivity, as seen through the psychoanalytic perspective, is an obvious and fundamental paradox – that psychoanalysis has shown that many of our most human aspects, which make us passionate, vulnerable, and problematic beings, reside in our unconscious and often appear to us as if they came from somewhere else, from an 'It,' Freud's *das Es*. We may experience this core of our being – as Freud[6] described the unconscious wishful impulses embedded in the unconscious – as a place outside ourselves in some way, in some objective place, certainly in some other location. Even when we begin to discuss in a formal way the nature of this subjectivity, something always gets lost; we too readily fall into an objective way of thinking, where we may lose the heart of who we are. At the same time, this dilemma highlights what Husserl called the paradox of human subjectivity,[7] the fact that the human being is both a subject for the world, and at the same time, an object in the world.

I would further suggest that there are at least three main ways of looking at the term *subject* in philosophy, and these meanings provide the backdrop to the psychoanalytic way of looking at the term. First, there is the notion, going back to the ancient Greeks, of the subject as an underlying entity, a foundation, a unity underlying the multiplicity of phenomena, what they called the *hypokeimenon*. This then became translated in Latin into the *subjectum*: that which lies under or near, that which borders on something. The term *subject,* derived from the Latin, still seems to keep some notion of an underlying foundation. Descartes transformed this founding entity into the I think as the ultimate authority about what we know to be certain. There were then thinking subjects perceiving external objects, and hence evolved the subject – object dichotomy, which has dominated much thinking about the mind ever since.

Even when the objects are placed within the mind itself, as in object-relations theory, the model used is still very much a Cartesian one, based on a subject-object dichotomy. The danger with this way of thinking is that the subject can become an isolated entity, only certain of its own inner workings, cut off from the social field.

A second stream of philosophical thought, which seems to originate with Hume, offers a much more elusive and fragmentary notion of the subject and, indeed, has probably become the guiding model for contemporary postmodern thought.

Hume denied that there was any underlying self or subject; instead, we are simply a collection of different perceptions, a theatre where perceptions come and go:

> For my part, when I enter most intimately into what I call myself, I always stumble on some particular perception or other, of heat or cold, light or shade, love or hatred, pain or pleasure. I never can catch my self at any time without a perception, and never can observe any thing but a perception ... [I] venture to affirm that [mankind is] nothing but a bundle or collection of different perceptions, which succeed each other with an inconceivable rapidity, and are in a perpetual flux and movement—The mind is a kind of theatre, where several perceptions successively make their appearance; pass, re-pass, glide away, and mingle in an infinite variety of postures and situations.[8]

It was partly in response to Hume's scepticism about an underlying subject that Kant developed his own philosophy, positing the synthetic function of the I think. The consciousness that accompanies different representations is still fragmentary and disunited, but when one joins one representation to another, through the synthetic function of imagination, the subject finds a sense of identity.[9]

However, it is with Nietzsche that one reaches the truly modern, not to say postmodern. For him,

> The "subject" is not something given, it is something added and invented and projected behind what there is ... [It is the] term for our belief in a unity underlying all the different impulses of the highest feeling of reality: we understand this belief as the effect of one cause — we believe so firmly in our belief that for its sake we imagine "truth," "reality," "substantiality" in general. "The subject" is the fiction that many similar states in us are the effect of one substratum: but it is we who first created the similarity of these states; our adjusting them and making them similar is the fact, not their similarity ... The sphere of a subject [is] constantly growing or decreasing, the centre of the system constantly shifting ... The assumption of one single subject is perhaps unnecessary; perhaps it is just as permissible to assume a multiplicity of subjects, whose interaction and struggle is the basis of our though.[10]

Thus, one can already see in Nietzsche's thought many of the contemporary preoccupations with the multiplicity of subjective viewpoints, the absence of a unified sense of subjectivity, the shifting centre of a system of thought, and the notion that subjectivity is not a given but is created.

For the sake of completeness, one can define a third trend in philosophical thought that comes from the Ancient Greeks, as interpreted by Heidegger. Instead of a subject-object dichotomy, he proposed a completely different axis of interpretation, involving the founding notion of Being, a concept he believed had been ignored ever since Greek thought was translated into Latin. If we posit the 'I' or subject as given, then he argued, one misses the importance of Being, which becomes revealed in our encounters with the world and with other beings.[11] While Heidegger's thought is both highly complex and fascinating, I leave it aside in this chapter as it does seem to push the field of enquiry into territory that needs separate consideration and may not be directly relevant to the theme of the chapter. Indeed, I would suggest that the first two models of the human subject currently inform and intertwine with much of current psychoanalytic thinking.

The Location of Human Subjectivity

A further philosophical issue, which is linked to the above considerations of the human subject, particularly those of Nietzsche, and which underpins much of psychoanalytic thought, is the question of the location of human subjectivity.

On the one hand, there is the notion, following Descartes, that the essence of human subjectivity is located inside the person, in the 'I think.' On the other hand, there is the counterargument, made by Hume and then Nietzsche, that there is no privileged place where unity is found. Indeed, Freud himself, in *The Interpretation of Dreams,* came up with an image of the mental apparatus that highlighted this very issue. To capture the way in which the mental apparatus functioned, he disregarded any notion of anatomical locality; instead, he pictured the apparatus as a compound microscope or a photographic instrument.

> On that basis, psychical locality will correspond to a point inside the apparatus at which one of the preliminary stages of an image comes into being. In the microscope and telescope, as we know, these occur in part at idea points, regions in which no tangible component of the apparatus is situated.[12]

Freud's metaphor suggests that there is something essentially elusive about our subjective life that makes it difficult to capture. The quest for the human 'centre,' where one can capture the origin of the person, is reminiscent of the search for the locus of the 'soul,' or for the place where consciousness resides, or where memory or language is centrally organized by the brain. Such quests proved fruitless until the search for the centre was abandoned in favour of an 'interactional' model, where a function is produced as a result of interaction between many elements or pathways, both within the subject and in relations between subjects, with no one place where everything comes together. Such an approach to the nature of the person is fundamentally different from that which starts out from the individual mind, isolated from other minds, as with Descartes. The latter produced a form of subjectivity that is free-floating, in the sense of being cut off from the social world, for only that kind of knowledge formed by the solitary Cartesian ego is certain. Freud's thought at times adheres to this form of thinking yet there often seems to be a pull towards another kind of thinking, which takes account of the fleeting and ambiguous nature of our subjective life as it exists in relation to a world of other subjects, and which cannot be tied down to the centralized and solitary ego.

There is thus an ambiguity about the nature of psychic locality and hence of subjectivity – whether it makes sense to locate the subject in the individual, in the social field, somewhere between, or, I would suggest, at some shifting position, involving both individual and social fields. Benjamin has also tackled this kind of issue from a psychoanalytical viewpoint. She considers the distinction between intrapsychic and intersubjective positions, and yet she points to the need to use a model of the mind that incorporates both positions without privileging either. Furthermore, she suggests that 'the analytic relationship provides some experience with the kind of intersubjective space that allows us to hold multiple positions.'[13]

Fonagy has approached these issues from a developmental perspective. He maintains that 'our understanding of the mental world is not a given, is radically different in the young child and crucially depends for its healthy development on interaction with other people who are sufficiently benign and reflective.'[14] Significantly, he cites the philosopher Marcia Cavell[15] as providing the philosophical demonstration of this basic position. Thinking for him is inherently intersubjective, requiring relationships between subjects for the individual to develop a capacity for self-reflection.

Lacan offered a more radical view of the human subject, who for him was essentially alienated, 'lacking' and 'fading.'[16] There is no place in his theory for a unified sense of who we are: subject and other are inextricably linked; when the subject appears in one place, he disappears in another. For Lacan, the unconscious appears through a split in the subject, so that the subject is always surprised by what then appears.

I would suggest that subjectivity incorporates both intrapsychic and intersubjective positions, both phenomena within the subject and between subjects in the social field. Psychoanalysis has mainly clarified intrapsychic phenomena and is only now paying more attention to the intersubjective arena. I am not implying that we should abandon the intrapsychic, for that would be to deny an essential component of the subject.

The Subject and Desire

An additional, though no less important, issue concerning the human subject is that of human desire and the relationship between knowledge and desire. This issue can be summarized as the difference between the 'cogni-tive' or 'knowing' subject and the 'desiring subject.' Dilthey highlighted the limitations of considering a merely knowing subject when he wrote that most philosophers

> ...had explained experience and cognition in terms of facts that are merely representational. No real blood flows in the veins of the know-ing subject constructed by Locke, Hume and Kant, but rather the diluted extract of reason as a mere activity of thought.[17]

Dilthey went on to consider the other aspects of the subject, including will-ing and feeling, and to maintain the importance for the subject of what he called the 'lived experience' of the subject, which became incorporated into subsequent thinkers – for example, in Husserl there was the 'life-world' and, in Habermas, the structure of the life-world in intersubjective communica-tion. But the latter thinkers do not pay much attention to human desire as such. It is in Hegel, as interpreted by the French thinker Kojève, that the issue of the desiring subject in relationship to the other arose, and in a form that is particularly relevant for psychoanalysis, as Lacan observed, Kojève[18] emphasized that the person who contemplates and is absorbed by what he contemplates, that is, the 'knowing subject,' only finds a particular kind of knowledge, knowledge of the object. To find the subject, desire is needed; the desiring subject is the human subject. As explored by Kojève, what is essentially human about desire is that the subject desires not just an object, not even the body, but the other's desire. One desires the other's desire. The movement between the subject and the other in a constant search for recogni-tion of their desires constitutes human reality. Desire is the essential element reaching beyond the individual subject to the other subject. These descrip-tions seem to capture an important element of the psychoanalytic relation-ship, in which the subject's desires, or wishes, dreams, and fantasies are the material on which analyst and patient work.

Relevant, too, in this context, is the thought of Benjamin, who, while considering the nature of femininity, asks what it means to be a subject, in particular a subject of desire.[19] She contends that sexual subjectivity is consti-tuted by being able to own desire, contain excitement, and hold it inside the body, rather than evacuating it immediately through discharge. I would add that, with anorexics and bulimics, one can see the opposite of this ability to own desire; it was very much an issue with the patient whose case I shall be presenting.

The Subject and Psychoanalysis

Having outlined some of the basic issues concerned with what we mean by the term subject, I shall now turn more directly to how they may be rel-evant for psychoanalysis. I begin with Freud's discoveries, which one could describe as being very much about bringing back elements of the mind, such as dreams and fantasies, into the realm of the human subject, when these, before him, had often been devalued as either mere fancies of no consequence or as inhabiting some kind of objective knowledge. Hence, becoming a subject would entail a process of recovery, or discovery, of unconscious subjective elements. It would also involve a complex mixture of conscious and unconscious elements.

Furthermore, the analytic setting itself, with the analyst sitting behind the patient, out of sight and reach, demonstrates literally that the analytic relationship is not an object relationship in the usual sense. With the analyst not being directly available, the analytic setting sets in motion a complex search for the human subject.

What I mean by this is that the patient brings to us all sorts of different stories, fixed patterns of relating or symptoms, hopes, expectations, and resistances. Patients often come with a sense of isolation; of either being alone with suffering or suffering from being alone. And they come to analysis, subject to various forces in their life, past and present. If the analysis works, then there is the possibility of their becoming the subject of their experiences and ultimately of their lives, with a sense of being no longer isolated and more in contact with others. Becoming a subject, then, involves a shift towards a *subjective position*. What I mean by this is that the term *subjective position* refers to how being a subject involves some capacity to take up different positions without their becoming fixed in a kind of frozen state of being. (Again, this is similar to Benjamin's attention to multiple positions, referred to above.) Being the subject of actions and thoughts is different from being subject to them or being in an 'objective position' where actions and thoughts and so on are not felt to be part of the subject's life. In order to be fully in touch with another person, in a truly subjective position, one begins to grasp the other's point of view; the other is seen as other, a person or a subject, in a context, orientated to others and being affected by others in the social world. A subjective position involves allowing experiences of the other, at many levels, conscious and unconscious, to interpenetrate oneself, so that they make an impact.

In the analytic encounter, the analyst may have to bear being in several different subjective positions in the session, rather than allowing himself to become fixed in one place, although at any moment he may find himself 'moored' in one place more favoured than another. I would suggest that the analyst's free-floating attention consists in a subjective oscillation between different positions or moorings. This means having to tolerate a considerable amount of ambiguity, uncertainty, and paradox. This situation involves difficulties for patients, such as the patient I shall describe, for whom uncertainty is very difficult to tolerate. For example, they may find the analyst's openness to the unconscious both a challenge and, at times, confusing.

In any shift towards a subjective position, or in becoming a subject, there is often a simultaneous move towards an objective position. That is, when we try to encounter the other fully as subject, we are often taken away to the other as mere object, i.e., with little sense of otherness, and we are constantly shifting between these two positions. In the patient I shall describe, there was a fundamental difficulty in allowing experiences of the other to make an impact.

Her body was often used to deflect away from experiencing the other and became almost objectified. Although I am suggesting that there are two basic and interacting positions in this clinical context, I would like to add here that there is a great deal of further complexity with regard to the terms *subjectivity* and *objectivity*. There are many different views of what we mean by an objective as opposed to a subjective understanding of human beings, even though I have proposed a specific use of these terms in the clinical setting. Thus Britton[20] drew attention to the fear in some patients of a conjunction of desire and subjectivity with a 'third object' of knowledge and objectivity. Such a conjunction may produce malignant understanding personified in the combined parental object. Britton also cites the work of the philosopher John Searle, who has pointed out how difficult it is to capture subjectivity, or the first-person point of view, with the usual objective language of natural science.[21] There is currently a great deal of philosophy of mind based on the thought of George Lakoff, whose seminal work was *Metaphors We Live By*, written in conjunction with Mark Johnson.[22] There it is argued that it is a myth to use either of the terms subjectivity or objectivity in the usual sense, without realizing that they fail to convey the way in which we understand the world through our interactions with it, particularly through the use of metaphorical thought. Thomas Nagel aimed to combine the subjective and objective viewpoints. He aimed to show how the interplay of these different views can be unified at certain times and then are also irreconcilable. He also cautions that the distinction between more subjective and more objective views is really a matter of degree and covers a wide spectrum.[23]

There is some similarity between what I am suggesting and the thought of Buber, who makes the distinction between two fundamental attitudes of living, which use two different pairs of words *I-Thou and I-It*. The *I* of the *I-Thou* appears as a person and becomes conscious of himself or herself as subjectivity. But while participation with others always remains a possibility, so does the I-It relationship and detachment. The realm of subjectivity includes both association and detachment.[24] One could further divide thinkers into those who veer more towards emphasizing objective understanding, e.g., taking a natural-science approach; those who emphasize the pre-eminence of subjective understanding, such as Kierkegaard;[25] those who try to eliminate the distinction, such as Dewey;[26] and, more recently, those like Rorty[27] and Nagel, who try to combine the two in some way. My own use of these terms, however, is rather pragmatic, and I aim to capture something essential in the analytic encounter.

In his paper 'The use of an object,'[28] Winnicott describes an important shift in relating that matches what I am trying to grasp. He describes 'object-relating,' which refers to a situation when the subject is an isolate. At this level, the individual subject functions omnipotently. Winnicott describes a more mature level of functioning, where the subject can use an object. The change from relating to using involves a particular process in which the subject destroys the object, but the object survives the destruction. Once the object has survived, the subject moves into a new kind of position, in which he can start to live in the world of objects, which can then be used and, therefore, the subject can have genuine contact with others. Thus, a subjective position involves the subject having real contact with his objects.

This way of thinking analytically, based on Winnicott's ideas, seems to have some parallels with subsequent Kleinian thinkers, such as Joseph,[29] who look for times when the patient and analyst go through moments of contact and loss of contact with one another. However, the language used in conceptualizing such moments, with, for example, the use of different kinds of projective identification, is different. Yet the kind of description of how psychic events can be organized has similarities with that of Klein's notion of the shift between paranoid-schizoid and depressive positions. However, there is a different emphasis; for example, I would suggest that the paranoid-schizoid position is an essentially pathological development, a good description of what happens in adult schizoid patients, but not necessarily relevant to all patients. As Stern has discussed,[30] there are fundamental difficulties with reconciling this theory with empirical findings from infant research. What I think is particularly novel in Klein's thinking is not only the way in which objects are said to be experienced as a unity in the depressive position and as a diversity in the paranoid-schizoid position, but also how the subjects who do the experiencing go in and out of different structural positions throughout their life. One may disagree with what these positions are exactly, but Klein gave us the structure for a new kind of thinking about the mind.

For Ogden, 'Central among the irreducible elements that define a psychoanalytic understanding of man is Freud's conception of the subject, and yet this theme remained a largely implicit one in Freud's writing. The Freudian conception of the process by which the subject is constituted is fundamentally dialectical in nature and involves the notion that the subject is created and sustained (and at the same time decentred from itself) through the dialectical interplay of consciousness and unconsciousness.'[31]

I would consider the notion of decentring, which follows from Freud's overturning of the dominant place of conscious reason in the life of the subject in favour of the unconscious, to be fundamental in understanding subjectivity in the psychoanalytic sense. The structure of the subject always involves an essential decentring. Or put another way, the subject has no central self in the sense of trying to fill in the vacuum, or gap, created by the decentred subject. Without the decentring there would be no unconscious.

Intersubjectivity as a central concept has also been used by, for example, Stolorow and his colleagues,[32] who use it as a framework for a theory of relatedness. For them, intersubjectivity provides the essential context for relating. There is an emphasis on the mutual and reciprocal interplay of subjective worlds, including that of the analyst, in an intersubjective 'field.' It is also worth adding that 'intersubjective relatedness' is essentially a term borrowed from infant researchers such as Stern. It refers to that important time when the child becomes orientated towards the other and begins to have an ability to share experiences. The other is seen as having a mind of his or her own, with which experiences can be shared. Fonagy and Target have also called this a process of 'mentalization,' when the child begins to have an idea of the other's mind. While I agree that this is an important concept, I consider that it only points to one area of relations between adult subjects. When I use the term *subject*, it may incorporate infantile elements, but the term essentially refers to the complex nature of the adult, with all the layers of experience, history, and ambiguity that have accumulated. Intersubjectivity thus refers not only to the sharing of experiences but also to issues of meaning surrounding these relations, the nature of the orientation to the other, how one understands the other and is affected by the other, and the place of human desire, as well as the nature of the social world.

One could ask why it is necessary to use the term *subject* rather than, say, *self* to describe the human individual in analysis. I would answer that the term is useful as a way of capturing many shades of meaning concerning the psychoanalytic field. I have already indicated that the term *subject*, at least in English, captures a basic dual aspect of the human situation, that we are both subject of and subject to various phenomena. I do not think that the term *self* has at its disposal these sorts of resonances of meaning, which make the use of the term *subject* so rich for theoretical construction. In addition, *self* tends to imply a filled centre, rather than an ambiguous or elusive centre. However, the use of *self* has the advantage of capturing the ordinary emotional quality of human life. We talk of self-awareness, self-expression, a sense of self, and so on.

While it is often used as a psychoanalytic term, Mitchell points out that

> the most striking thing about the concept of self within current psychoanalytic thought is precisely the striking contrast between the centrality of concern with the self and the enormous variability and lack of consensus about what the term even means.[33]

Yet it is a term that seems more responsive to the ordinary human aspects of the person, while the term *subject* does suffer in this regard from having philosophical resonances. One solution to this dilemma is to use the term *self* primarily to describe the affective, responsive, experiencing side or element of the human subject. Indeed, I think that there can be self-experiences with little subjectivity. What I have in mind are certain patients who report the day's experiences in the session over and over, yet it is very difficult to make sense of what has happened to them. There may be little sense of a subject of these experiences, little sense that experiences have psychic value. Things are reported but not then reflected on or put into any context, and it is difficult for the analyst to interpret what has been happening. The session is rather like a news bulletin: raw news from the self but not commentary.

It is the work of Christopher Bollas that most closely matches the model of subjectivity that I have proposed. He coined the term *subject relations* to capture the nature of subjective experience in the analytic encounter. For him, this represents the complex interplay between the subjectivities of analyst and patient. While object relations theory attends to the formation and projection of self and object representations, subject relations theory attends to 'the interplay of two human sensibilities, who together create environments unique to their cohabitation.'[34]

What I wish to explore here is how we can begin to understand, in the interplay between sensibilities, how a shift to a subjective position comes about, and what is the nature of the shift, as well as who shifts and where. One can also ask whether or not shifting always involves both analyst and patient. Can there ever be change without the analyst changing in some essential way? Is there always mutual change? These questions, as well as contributions from several thinkers I have referred to above, point towards the inevitable linking of subject and other. Indeed, one could say that perceiving or taking account of one's life as another is the essential element needed to acquire a 'full' sense of subjectivity, one that is not encapsulated in an isolated position. That is, becoming a subject entails taking account of oneself as other in some way. Or, as I have already indicated, becoming a subject involves both the intrapsychic and intersubjective fields.

Obviously, in the analytic situation, such taking account mainly occurs through speaking, through sharing experiences, and having some sort of dialogue with the other. Becoming a subject would imply being in a position to share in this way with the other, something which the patient I shall describe found particularly difficult.

My overall picture of this field of enquiry is that the human subject is essentially elusive, appearing and disappearing as subject and other come together or fail to connect. One may capture the subject in the analytic encounter, mainly through speaking, but still, something vital always escapes. Bion was very much exercised with this kind of problem. To understand the patient's statements, he devised a complicated grid to capture the patient's statements as transformations. Yet, as he advised in *Attention and Interpretation*,[35] such acts of understanding could also intrude on an analytic session itself. Thus, it is difficult to describe what happens in the analytic encounter without losing something essential, because such descriptions necessarily entail taking up some kind of observing position outside what is going on between analyst and patient. Indeed, the patient may try to keep the analyst in that kind of position, as with the patient I shall describe below. No doubt a certain amount of observing is a prerequisite for understanding what is going on between analyst and patient. The problem arises when this dominates. There is also the point that, as in physics, observing always shifts the perspective; there is no observation without an effect on the participants. It is this effect that is of particular interest to the psychoanalyst. Furthermore, the fact that the subjective positions of analyst and patient are different does not necessarily imply that there cannot be some mutuality. Indeed, in the clinical example I shall give, it was when I felt very much left out in the cold, with no mutuality, that I intervened to try to shift the situation. We, as analysts, try to use the asymmetry or overcome it, but we cannot ignore it. Indeed, although the analytic relationship is an intimate one, it is also a fundamentally distorted one, where the subjectivities of analyst and patient are not at the same level; the patient's world is to be examined in the open, while the analyst's is essentially masked, except at a few contact points with the patient. However, how the mask may be lifted or not may have important bearings on the analysis. The analyst has a mask-like function, or role, as he is out of sight; the patient's ordinary defences are then undermined, and there is potentially greater access to the unconscious. One is reminded in this context of the fact that one of the uses of the mask in Greek theatre was to make the voice heard by the audience, hiding the face of the actor yet revealing the deep truths of the poet. This is not to say that the analyst only wears a mask; he may reveal his human aspects, but this takes place in a context in which he appears and disappears from behind the mask. In the clinical example, I hope to convey a moment when, as it were, I stepped out from behind the mask in order to make an intervention that seemed to be necessary. That is, the analyst is essentially elusive, mirroring and recreating the essential nature of subjectivity. Without the mask, psychoanalysis cannot take place. That is, the analytic relationship arises out of the difference in subjective positions of analyst and patient. Out of the gaps, perplexing difficulties or 'aporias' between analyst and patient arise, all sorts of problems and possibilities.

But what takes place is often difficult to describe. It can be difficult to know what takes place and where. I suggest that things take place in various shifting positions between analyst and patient, where the subject opens up or closes down. This shifting provides the basis for human subjectivity. Becoming a subject involves some sort of opening up, but one cannot ignore the closing down. Thus I have referred to two kinds of processes in this context, in the interplay of sensibilities: appearing and disappearing, opening up and closing down. Of course, there are no doubt other kinds of processes that need to be explored.

Clinical Example

I shall describe some work with a patient for whom opening up to the subjective realm was particularly difficult, as she used and abused her body, which persistently took her away from communicating with others and kept her, in some ways, in an almost objectified state. Mrs. A has not needed hospital admission for her problems because of her family support and basic resilience, but she reveals symptoms that one often sees in the hospitalized self-harming patient. She often remains in her private world, while having difficulty in moving into a subjective position, relating to other subjects and sharing experiences. She has difficulty with what I have called 'taking oneself as another.' It was when I began to experience the impact on me of that situation, that is, that I was nowhere to be found as a subject in the session except as some disembodied and unreal entity, that something shifted. I think that work with her, which I should add has often been highly problematic, highlights, in rather an extreme way, some of the kinds of issues concerning the nature of our subjective life that I have raised above. For example, not only the issue of otherness being a part of subjectivity, but also that subjectivity implies some moving between positions, as well as a process of a reasonable amount of opening up to the other, however elusive the subject ultimately is. What I describe is something about the effect on me of her way of relating, that is, her impact on me and how I have tried to use this in the service of her analysis.

Mrs. A, who was in her mid-1930s and married with a family, presented a long history of severe eating problems – anorexia, bulimia, and self-harm. Ever since childhood, she has binged and vomited and has attacked her body in various ways, cutting and scratching herself. She would binge on what I have called 'bad food,' such as dog biscuits and mouldy cheese. Her early self-harm used to fool doctors by creating false medical conditions, for example, by picking at a finger so that it looked like a fungal infection. She would also rub dirt into cuts in order to prolong and worsen the wound. From childhood, she had created a secret world, cut off from others, which she continued to use into adult life as a way of retreating from others and providing some sort of comfort. This secret world, which seems to be a mixture of conscious and unconscious elements, is experienced as important to her; it is where she finds her sense of identity, however precarious, and it gives her a sense of belonging to a world of other people with similar problems. Yet there is something highly problematic about her use of this world, which cuts her off from close and intimate contact with others. That is, there is in it little sense of the notion of a subject because there is almost no sense of otherness. She gave me glimpses of this private world, but it was often difficult to be in touch with her, partly as a result of conscious resistance and a fear of losing control, and partly because her private world sustained her for so long. Indeed, it was only well into her adult life that she began to realize that there was something worrying that needed attention, for she had managed to fool herself, as earlier on she had her doctors, into believing that there was nothing wrong.

However, in the analysis, she showed at times a courageous attempt to face her denials. She often remarked that she just had to face the truth in analysis, even though she often reacted to insight by harming herself. That is, there was the basic wish to relate to the other, however difficult. There was some search for a subject, however precarious.

She comes from a middle-class background. Her father is described as being intrusive and too seductive with her. She found it difficult talking about her relationship with him as it had hints of being sexualized. She retained a strong masculine identification, but at times felt she did not belong to any sex. Her fantasy of an ideal body would be basically thin and masculine-looking.

The mother is described as being undemonstrative, not particularly comfortable about being feminine, and mechanical in her mothering, though a strong character and a homemaker.

She felt that, in a way, her father was more maternal. As came out in a session, from the transference experience, he appeared to be the one with the breasts, more like the primary object.

Her adolescence was a stormy time. Apart from her eating problems, she also became quite promiscuous for a while as a way of trying to prove herself to be feminine. She has a long-standing marriage to a husband who is described as unresponsive yet also long-suffering. He did not wish to hear about her problems, which caused her considerable frustration. She is a devoted mother, though she feels very guilty about how she treated her children as babies and fears she has damaged them, as she withheld food from herself and from them when they were born.

The analysis, some years ago, was not easy. Productive sessions were often followed by destructive activity and an accompanying forgetting of what took place. Despite at times considerable resistance to talking and sharing, she continued to come; when I fed her, as it were, she repeatedly got rid of what I had offered, as is common with bulimic patients. However, despite all this, she had a kind of gutsy attitude to life, and cared for people, though unfortunately not too much for herself.

Mrs. A described constant states of emptiness and fullness. She often described herself as a tube of toothpaste whose contents had to be squeezed out. This description was accompanied by a wish to lose herself, i.e., to have no sense of being a subject. In one session, she came out with the phrase 'mental bulimia' to describe how she fills herself up and empties her mind and said that the bulimic way of relating was like a straitjacket, limiting her freedom and, I would add, her sense of being a subject of her actions. These states are similar to those described by Benjamin (1998, pp. 76–77), to which I have already referred, when she discusses the nature of the subject's desire, and the need for ownership of desires. That is, Mrs. A had difficulty in containing and holding desire.

I will describe two fairly typical sessions, which aim to give a picture of what it was like being with my patient.

First session:

This was a Tuesday session, mid-term. She said that she had been to her doctor, who had diagnosed a chest infection. She had been feeling physically bad for the last few days, but she was confused about everything, what was physical and what was mental. 'Was my chest infection real?' she asked herself. This was a somatic theme that had come up on a number of occasions in the previous few sessions, which had increasingly made her express doubts about being in analysis. There were obvious links with the way that she had fooled doctors as a child, which had then given her a vast sense of omnipotence but had also left her feeling desperately alone, as no one understood her; she was now left feeling confused about what was real and what was a fiction. Although she had been coughing a lot and the doctor had prescribed antibiotics, she still thought that she might have fooled him without knowing it.

Before I had time to link this material with me, she railed against her husband for not wanting to listen to her, for not wanting to know about her cutting and bingeing, and then about men in general. 'Including me,' I added. She agreed and continued to complain about men, who never understand, unlike her female friends with whom she can share. This theme continued for some time. Leaving aside the fact that female friendships can be very intimate, I was feeling battered again, as I had been feeling from time to time in the previous few sessions, as well as on many other occasions. I knew from then that there was little I could do to intervene effectively. Interpretations of content generally led nowhere, and we could easily have got into a sterile examination of what was real and what was not. I then suddenly had the thought that what was real was that she seemed to have absolutely no idea of the effect or impact she had on me, not to mention my dilemma about how to respond. I then said, with a certain amount of curiosity: 'I wonder what it is you think I didn't understand?'

She replied by complaining about my lack of response: I did not say enough (which was possibly true); I was too silent; she did not know what to do. She was still cutting herself, so nothing was helping. But then she quickly added that, really, she would like to be silent here and for me to do all the talking. She knew that this was stupid, but all the same, it was what she wanted, and why was it so unreasonable?

I did wonder why I did not speak as much as I might have. I have rather a laconic style; I tend to wait before saying that much, and then actively get engaged with the patient from time to time. And yet what she said about wanting me to fill the space was so unrealistic that I felt that this was the time to intervene. I decided to come out from behind the mask, as it were, and to share with her my own frustration, but I hoped in a way that would make sense. I said that it was indeed difficult to know how to respond to her, as her talk was so often – as it had begun to be again today – about her body and her cutting. I added that her imperviousness was very difficult to penetrate, so that it was difficult for me to know how to reach her.

Slightly to my surprise, she readily agreed with this and said that, in fact, her friends always said this. They never knew what she really thought, which frustrated them. (I did then wonder why I had waited so long before coming up with my observation about my difficulty in responding.) I made some comment about analysis trying to sort this issue out. But she added that analyzing only made things worse. She was aware of fighting me, though she did see that, at least in the outside world, she was freed up more. Friends had commented on her improvement. But there were also times when she felt much worse. Her self-harm was escalating. She then went on to talk about the body, about differences between men and women, about which, we established, she felt very confused. Ideally, she wanted to be androgynous. She was not certain about how different she was from men and how similar to them. The body and the skin also confused her: what the skin was for and how it contained the body. At some point here, I talked about a psychological space that could make sense of all this confusion, removing this preoccupation with mere bodily functions. She added that it was the skin that held together the body.

The main anxiety of the session then seemed to me to become clear. I interpreted that there was also a holding together in a psychological sense. She had come to the session feeling that her body was falling apart with the chest infection. But she was also falling apart in her mind. She was probably wondering whether or not I could hold things together and whether I could understand her, rather than be fooled by her. This made sense to her.

Finally, there was some discussion about how she might be able to use me to sort things out, but she could not bear to do that because I was like all the other men who did not listen and were unresponsive and so on. Thus by the end of the session, the issue of how to establish ordinary mutuality had at least come to the fore. There was some sharing, some sense of engagement between subject and other.

Comments on the first session:

On the one hand, it was difficult to make contact with Mrs. A, and yet, on the other, it was possible to do so. She was constantly struggling with her wish to get lost in her body; there was a real confusion between body and mind. There was an issue about how willful she was, how much she might hide from me or try to fool me, as a kind of seductive game in which I had to find her. I was let in, to some extent, but only so far. One could say that this reflected the nature of her subjective life; there was a little opening up, but a quick closing down. Sharing of thoughts was minimal; awareness of otherness was restricted. Perhaps there was also the issue about the nature of my holding function. Was my skin still intact, as it were, after all the complaints and 'cutting' remarks at the beginning of the session? I certainly did feel that using my experience of being excluded and then feeding this back to her made an impact, which in turn allowed some opening up. As it was the only thing about which I was certain, it perhaps led to some genuine shift.

Central to what took place with Mrs. A was the issue of the analyst's responsiveness, which she herself complained about as being inadequate. It was only when I took what she said seriously, but also began to wonder what effect she was having on my ordinary responsiveness, that the session could move away from the body-centred material into something more concerned with her subjective life. It was then that her complaints about men, which seemed to be mainly complaints about difference, including those between her and me, moved into the deeper material concerned with her skin problems, and how she could stay inside her skin without cutting it. The interpretation I made about her imperviousness was an attempt to move the analytic discourse from a kind of monologue into the intersubjective realm where there might be more dialogue. At this point, I could make what felt like a familiar and more traditional analytic interpretation about holding and falling apart. Some similar issues returned in the following session.

Second session:

This was a Monday session soon after the previous session. Mrs. A was feeling very downhill at the weekend. She had binged and cut on several occasions. She felt like a heap. 'Is it worth talking,' she continued, 'as it only makes me worse?' I made some remark about the fact that there had been a break in the talking here over the weekend. She did not obviously respond to this but continued by saying that she had had thoughts of suicide; however, the children had kept her from it. There were moments when she thought she needed a rest from it all. She admitted going to her doctor, who had increased her dose of antidepressants (which she has taken on and off).

She then said that her son had been involved in some kind of cutting game at school. She was afraid that he might have seen her cutting herself through the bathroom keyhole. She told him fiercely not to play such games again. She wondered whether he was an extension of her, so had picked up her problems. She then mentioned that someone at her work had mocked her. In fact, this was fairly mild, but she had such a low opinion of herself, despite her success there, that she thought they were right to mock her. This made her have thoughts about her father, who called her his beautiful daughter, even though she was clearly plain. This was a big issue for her. Though fathers may adore daughters, his unrealistic and over-close flattery of her merely made a mockery of her. Thinking rather along the lines of the first session, with regard to her impact on me and mine on her (that is, on the interaction between our two different subjective positions), I wondered whether she had thoughts about how I saw her. She replied that she tried to put such thoughts out of her mind. This was a strange kind of relationship, being on the couch; it was not a real one. She then returned to thoughts about her bad weekend for a while.

I suggested that she might be mocking herself, her own capacities and achievements. When she achieved something, she often then reacted badly to it, as she did here. 'Maybe,' she replied. After a silence, she talked about some recent family events as well as quarrels with her husband about discipline of the children. She is more laid-back than he is with them and this causes disputes. I said that what she was saying was not only about how her father saw her but also about how she and men can get together, or not, in cooperation, as part of a couple for instance.

She then brought up her doctor who, despite knowing that she was in analysis, talked about sending her to an eating disorder unit.

I obviously was somewhat put out by this, though also rather amused. I felt that her doctor had panicked and had been taken in by her. I took up what she said in terms of her mocking me and her turning away from me to the doctor for help. It was like turning away from my food. But it was also something about the kind of interaction, or working together, we had. She might have wondered whether or not I could hear what she had to say and could tolerate it. This made her thoughtful and did lead in the next couple of sessions to further thoughts about how her cutting might have the effect of reducing the impact I had on her; it took her away from the sessions into her private, cut-off world. This happened especially when there was the possibility of taking something from me.

Comments on the second session:

There was quite a lot in this session about turning away from me and being indirectly angry with me, with her use of the doctor over the weekend. She had only rarely been directly angry with me; such open expression of feeling was very threatening for her. I wondered how much I was having to look through the keyhole at her, witnessing her perverse activity but being unable to influence it much. One could also wonder how much she could see anyone else as a subject; instead, they had to be audience or viewers of her body as a mere object. She feared her son was an extension of herself rather than a subject in his own right. This seemed to have connections with the father, who saw her as a mere phallic extension of himself, thus distorting her relationship to her own body and interfering with her capacity to become comfortable with feminine desire.

There were all kinds of allusions to sexuality, how much she saw herself as a woman, or, as later came out, as a woman in a man's body. This fantasy may be related to the maternal father with breasts, with whom she identifies, but also feels mocked. There were hints in this session, later confirmed, about her hatred of her feminine body, including the sites of her sexual desire, her breasts and vagina, which she also cut.

The session began with her despair, which had led to thoughts of suicide, but there was some willingness to look, through the interaction with me, at what was leading to the despair, for example, the mocking severance of contact with the other. Once again. I felt that the issue of her struggling to become a subject came to the fore by the end of the session. At least by then there was some recognition that she could take something from me. I was not as cut off as she imagined. It is possible that the difficulties brought up in this second session were produced by the revelations of the first session, rather than the weekend separation, which then produced a temporary regression. These very difficulties could have been a sign that there had been a successful shift in the analysis.

Concluding Remarks

I do believe that the analyst's attitude can deeply influence what goes on in analysis. How much elbowroom the analyst can allow the patient may be a major factor in allowing the patient to make changes. However, with my patient, I had constantly found my own freedom to manoeuvre curtailed. My lack of elbowroom was clearly related to her difficulty in shifting between different positions, the lack of flexibility in her psychic organization. She was often stuck in one main kind of position, her body-immersed organization. The blurring of differences, so that one may not know who was the subject in a session, as well as the use of cutting to close off meaningful communication, also made the analysis difficult. One could say that the cutting had become an addiction that wipes out meaning. It also gave Mrs. A the sense of being in charge of everything. The treatment of such patients can often be taxing for the analyst. I should add, however, that in her occupation she could be quite creative and, occasionally, her talents in this area came into the analysis. My patient was often taxing because of her constant closing up. She was so often subject to experiences, particularly organized around her body, and rarely the subject *of* her experiences. It is as if she herself, as a subject, peeps out and then quickly retreats into the apparent safety and yet confusion of her body-immersed organization. The confusion over the primary object may be relevant here, distorting her identifications. Indeed, one may wonder how she can ever inhabit a fully subjective world.

What also makes the analysis difficult is the concrete way in which Mrs. A often seemed to function. Thus, being with another person can feel literally like opening up in the physical rather than symbolic sense. I think that there are some similarities between this and the hysteric's use of the body. The hysteric uses the body to express a psychic conflict, while there is also a denial of sexual desire. Commenting on Freud's Dora case, Kohon[36] has also described how the hysteric remains a go-between, as a kind of object of exchange but not, I would add, a subject; from which follows that they cannot take up their own desire. Kohon describes how the hysteric shifts between mother and father, never being fixed in one position. I would see this process of shifting as different from a flexible form of shifting, where one can stay in one position and then move to another. There have been only rare moments in the analysis when I could reveal my ordinary human side or at least be more responsive.

Yet the moment that I finally realized that nothing I was saying seemed to be making any impact and could interpret this, the analysis shifted a little. Such moments, when the analyst suddenly has a thought that makes a difference, are obviously complex; a lot of preliminary listening precedes such moments. In Winnicott's terms, one has to survive the patient's need to destroy the analyst in order for them to move into a new position, as a subject who can use the other. Surviving the impact of the patient seems to be an essential part of holding.

Symington[37] describes a similar situation in analysis to that which I experienced with my patient when I began to face her impact on me. He contends that the analyst's inner act of freedom brings about a therapeutic shift in the patient; the patient perceives this inner act and change occurs. My musing about what I was experiencing certainly led to a sort of freeing up in the session. Parsons[38] also talks about mutative moments when analyst and patient suddenly find what really matters in the analysis. Both of them need to be taken by surprise and to let go of familiar ways of understanding. I described in an earlier paper[39] how the thought suddenly arose in me during a session that my obsessional patient had difficulty in dealing with a dual aspect of the transference, i.e., in seeing the analyst as both a real person and as a fantasy object. This thought, when shared with the patient, seemed to make a difference to the work of the analysis; it seemed to represent a pivotal moment in the analytic relationship, which had become rather stuck.

In the introduction, I raised the question about whether there can be any change in analysis that is not mutual in some way. I am not certain how, if at all, I have changed as a result of what happened in the analysis. I certainly had to shift my interventions in order to get through to Mrs. A. I also had to listen to her complaints about me and not dismiss them as mere evidence of resistance. Certainly the writing of the paper, and the various comments on it I have received from colleagues, helped me to clarify my thoughts both about subjectivity and the analysis.

Some patients rather quickly get the notion that sharing thoughts can be productive and that opening up can be rewarding as well as frightening. Free association can then be an exciting prospect. But with Mrs. A, free association was an enormous threat as she had basic difficulties with owning the products of her mind. Perhaps this difficulty was related to her body/mind confusion. In turn, I had difficulty in knowing how to respond, how to bridge our different subjective positions. I have argued that subjectivity is essentially elusive, that the subject appears and disappears, comes and goes. However, Mrs. A has demonstrated great difficulties in experiencing elusiveness, in registering presence and absence, as can be seen in the second session I described, where the weekend break might have led to the wiping out of the analysis. But the fact that we continued to wrestle with such basic difficulties may indicate that the analysis of such patients reveals, in an extreme form, something valuable about the analytic process, as seen from both sides of the couch.

Notes

1 Ogden (1992, p. 624).
2 Hoffman (1991, p. 624).
3 Berger and Luckmann (1966).
4 Benjamin (1988, 1998).
5 Benjamin (1998, p. 39).
6 Freud (1900, p. 603).
7 Husserl (1954, p. 178).
8 Hume (1740, pp. 252–253).
9 Kant (1934 [1787], p. 95).
10 Nietzsche (1968 [1901], pp. 267–270).
11 Heidegger (1962 [1926], p. 72).
12 Freud (1900, p. 536).
13 Benjamin (1998, p. 90).
14 Fonagy and Target (1996, p. 218).
15 Cavell (1991).
16 Benvenuto and Kennedy (1986).
17 Dilthey (1989 [1883], p. 50).
18 Kojève (1980 [1947], p. 3).
19 Benjamin (1998, p. 76).
20 Britton (1996).

21 Searle (1992, p. 98ff).
22 Lakoff and Johnson (1980).
23 Nagel (1986, p. 5).
24 Buber (1970, p. 113).
25 Kierkegaard (1941 [1846]).
26 Dewey (1929).
27 Rorty (1989).
28 Winnicott (1969).
29 Joseph (1989).
30 Stern (1985, p. 254).
31 Ogden (1994, p. 30).
32 Stolorow et al. (1994).
33 Mitchell (1991, p. 124).
34 Bollas (1989, pp. 108–109).
35 Bion (1970, p. 59).
36 Kohon (1984).
37 Symington (1983).
38 Parsons (1986).
39 Kennedy (1984).

3 Revisiting Subject Relations Theory

The philosopher Thomas Nagel describes how,

> Subjects of experience are not like anything else. While they do have observable properties, the most important thing about them is that they are subjects, and it is their subjective mental properties that must be explained if we are to be able to identify them with anything in the objective order.[1]

The philosopher Norman Malcolm wrote that,

> Human life contains many elements or stages: birth, childhood, family, life, schooling, sexual awakening, love, friendship, marriage, work, poverty, parenthood, ageing, illness, death. These destinies and vicissitudes are undergone and suffered by *people,* by you and me: not by immaterial minds or brains or machines. The human being who encounters these conditions is the *subject.*[2]

In trying to grasp himself and his own experience in his essays, or 'assays' or 'trials,' Montaigne described how he could not fix his subject.

> I cannot keep my subject still…I do not portray being: I portray passing…from minute to minute. My history needs to be adapted to the moment…This is a record of various and changeable occurrences…If my mind could gain a firm footing, I would not make essays… [I am] always in apprenticeship and on trial.[3]

In the 1990s, I tried to capture the complex issue of human subjectivity and its trials and tribulations within the psychoanalytic setting in a series of papers, two in Psychoanalytic Dialogues (1996,[4] 1997[5]) and one in the International Journal of Psychoanalysis (2000),[6] and in detail in a book, *The Elusive Human Subject* (1998).[7] I put forward a theory of subject relations, as an addition to psychoanalytic theory and practice. I should add that subject relations theory is *not* about the analyst self-disclosing, nor

DOI: 10.4324/9781003683315-3

does it entail a main focus on the ordinary relationship aspects of the analyst/patient encounter.

The term subject relations theory seems to have first been used by Christopher Bollas in 1989[8] to cover the interplay between the subjectivities of analyst and patient, but he does not develop this notion in much detail. He does, however, importantly sketch out what he calls 'Freudian Intersubjectivity,' which is distinct from the intersubjective approach of relational psychoanalysts. Returning to Freud, Bollas describes how the patient's free associations and the analyst's evenly suspended attention or what is often described now as a form of 'reverie' provides for the essential ingredients of the analytic intersubjective relationship, one which is asymmetrical, with limited self-disclosure by the analyst, and not to be confused with an ordinary relationship as seems to be the case with relational analysts, however much I would add the real relationship and the human aspects of the analytic encounter may also come into play. Continuing a line of thought that Bollas began, I tried to examine in detail the nature of analytic subjectivity, and how the subject may be looked at within the context of what I called for convenience a subjective organization. This is a loose and open term ranging from the personal and individual to what takes place between subjects in the social field, where subjects meet others in the network of other subjects.

I described the essence of the human subject as essentially elusive, appearing and disappearing as subject and other come together or fail to connect, and how failures or breakdowns of communication in analysis can be sources of insight and change. 'Becoming a subject' involves some form of opening up; but one cannot ignore the closing down in the psychoanalytic interplay of sensibilities. This does not mean that one cannot feel fully alive as a human subject, but it is a complex process as I hope to convey. What I am describing is also different from the states of mind of some patients who are difficult to understand, who have little firm identity or who are always disappearing from sight as it were; that's a different kind of elusiveness.

This notion of subjective elusiveness has been echoed subsequently by others, for example, by Shmuel Ehrlich, who wrote in 2003 that:

> The subject as an idea...can never be pinned down: it is never an 'is'. Always elusive, it remains forever a fantasy construct become experiential fact...As a frontier, it is the most difficult one to draw and specify: the simplest, intuitively most evident boundary is that drawn between subject and object, between self and other. Psychoanalysis has taught us, however, that this enticing simplicity is misleading...since the subject often recedes and disappears, finds itself decentered and is hardly the 'centre stage actor' it purports to be.[9]

The philosopher Roger Scruton captured what he described as the 'mystery' that arises from the view of the human subject.

> No attempt to pin down the subject in the world of objects will ever really succeed. You can extract form the person as many body parts as you will, but you will never find the place where he is, the place from which he addressed me and which I in turn address…It seems there is an impass-able metaphysical gap, between the human object, and the free subject to whom we relate as a person. Yet we constantly cross that gap.[10]

The French analyst René Roussillon wrote that,

> The accession to the true dimension of intersubjectivity cannot be gained without taking into account the intersubjectivity of this particu-lar aspect of the human subject: he has an inner shadowy and unknown zone; his messages contain a dimension that eludes him, an uncon-scious dimension that nevertheless acts and interacts between one sub-ject and another.[11]

French analysts, influenced by Lacan, as indeed I have been, as I shall come to later, have developed the notion of 'subjectivation' as a description of the process by which the subject emerges in the relationship with the other.[12]

Prior to my 1998 book, Ogden, who very much influenced my own think-ing, wrote that, 'the psychoanalytic theory of experiencing 'I-ness' must incorporate into its own structure and language a recognition of the inef-fable, constantly moving and evolving nature of subjectivity.'[13] He compares this to what Milan Kundera calls the 'unbearable lightness of being.'[14] He views the analytic process as one which creates the analytic subject who had not previously existed and which is in an ever-evolving state in the dynamic intersubjectivity of the analytic process. He also makes the point that the term 'self' is inadequate to convey the complexity of the human subject, tied as it is to the now discarded view of a centrally organized entity 'inside' the per-son. Whereas psychoanalysis reveals that the sense of 'I-ness' emerges from a 'continually decentering dialectical process.'

Decentering is a term that originally referred to the impact of Freud's 'Copernican' revolution, where consciousness and conscious reason were no longer the home of meaning, for the core of humankind's being was now placed elsewhere, in the unconscious as for example revealed in *The Inter-pretation of Dreams*. The issue of a central core in the subject is a difficult one. I would rather conceive of a complex organization in which the subject moves in and out of different positions over time, with some central coher-ence at various parts of the organization. These movements are reflected in the pattern of narratives encountered in an analytic session.

The subject also develops over time in complex ways. The psychoanalytic concept of development does not merely refer to processes involving linear time, or what I have called the 'history of events,' but also a different kind of time, the 'history of layers,'[15] where past and present are constantly being reorganized by the human subject. Overlapping stages of development are tied to the subject's history within the context of the developing child's attempt to place themselves within a family and societal structure and are also to be seen in the adult's subsequent reorganization of memory (après coup). The stages can be seen as nodes or turning points in the subject's attempts to recognize their history.[16]

At the heart of our subjectivity, as seen from the psychoanalytic perspective, is an obvious and fundamental paradox – that psychoanalysis has shown that many of our most human aspects, what makes us passionate, vulnerable, and problematic beings, reside in our unconscious, and often appear to us as if they came from somewhere else, from an 'I,' Das Es in Freud. We may experience this core of our being, as Freud[17] described the unconscious wishful impulses embedded in the unconscious, as a place outside ourselves in some way, in some objective place, certainly in some other location. Even when we begin to discuss in a formal way the nature of this subjectivity, something becomes lost. We too readily fall into an objective way of thinking, where we may lose the heart of who we are. At the same time, this dilemma highlights the paradox of human subjectivity: that the human being is both a subject for the world and at the same time an object in the world.

Freud also pointed out that there is always a point where we reach the unknown in the human subject. He was referring particularly to *The Interpretation of Dreams*, where we reach the 'dream's navel'[18] the spot where it reaches down into the unknown. But one could extend this notion to the possibility that there is always something unknowable and irreducible in the human subject, and hence something about us essentially difficult to describe.

The word 'self' is often used in descriptions of subjective states, and it has the advantage of capturing something of the emotional quality of human life. We talk of self-awareness, self-expression, self-reflection, and self-knowledge. The self in self-psychology is, 'that part of the personality which confers the sense of selfhood, and which is evoked and sustained by a constant supply of responsiveness from the functioning of selfobjects.'[19]

Stephen Mitchell[20] proposes an interesting model for understanding self-experience from different points of view. The self can be multiple and discontinuous, which refers to 'the multiple configurations of self-patterned variability in different relational contexts.'[21] Or the self can be separate, integral, and continuous, which refers to the 'subjective experience of the pattern making itself, activity that is experienced over time and across the different organizational schemes.'[22]

Philip Bromberg[23] offers an alternative description of a similar view when he suggests that 'health is the ability to stand between realities without losing any of them. This is what I believe self-acceptance means and what creativity is really all about – the capacity to feel like oneself while being many.'

Although these descriptions match my own thinking to some extent, I feel that we need to clarify how these single and multiple organizations are structured, particularly within other frameworks of thought, such as philosophy and sociology. Whatever the limits and uncertainties of the term self, it does seem more responsive to ordinary human aspects of the person, whereas the term subject suffers in this regard from having philosophical resonances. I would indeed emphasize that there is no perfect solution to the dilemma of human subjectivity, for terms always lose something essential in us. But I do feel that the term self is too loose for theoretical purposes and does not capture enough of our complexity. I would like to keep the term self somewhere, though, and I propose that it could be used to describe the affective, responsive, experiencing side or element of the human subject, one aspect of the subjective organization, separate from other aspects, such as the place of social structure, desire, and embodiment.

Subject relations have remained the basis of my analytic work, as well as much of what I have written subsequently. Thus, in the book *The Psychic Home* (2014), which examines the links between psychoanalysis, consciousness, and the human soul, I wrote that,

> There is considerable overlap between the realm of subjectivity and that of the soul territory. If human beings have a soul, then that implies a subject with a soul, the soul's owner. It is difficult to say I have a subject, but not that I have a soul. In ordinary language, one might talk of someone having soul, meaning that they are capable of deep feeling and responsiveness to others. A lack of soul implies a lack of humanity, callousness, or superficiality. The soul thus seems emblematic of deep subjective experience, which goes along with some ownership of that experience, and being marked by experience, allowing experience to impact on us in an alive way, so that the experience *takes root*.[24]

The notion of a psychic home, in which one can become rooted, described in detail in that book, seems to be a key organizer of intersubjective relationships.

Intersubjective relatedness is not only essential to understanding early mother-baby interactions, as described by Colwyn Trevarthen; it enables the synchrony of intentional rhythms, expressive gestural forms and qualities of voice which underlies 'communicative musicality' between infants and adults, one aspect of what makes music reach deeply into our subjective lives, as explored in detail in my book The Power of Music (2020). Music takes place in a virtual space between subjects. Though sounds are objective, music has a subjective reality. On the one hand, we hear sounds, but music makes particular use of sounds, which are organized by a human subject as a form of communication into an event. Listening to music, we enter into a musical world of human intention and agency. The physical sounds do not make music, do not give music its sense of movement; for example, the listening subject does that. Scruton describes how nothing *literally* moves in musical space, but in some way the idea of space cannot be eliminated from our experience of music. We are dealing with an entrenched metaphor embedded within our experience and cognition of music, which cannot be translated away by talking about the science of pitches, etc. Musical movement is a real presence.[25]

Analytic listening has many parallels with musical listening. The analyst listens to the patient's 'music,' thereby helping them 'give voice' to their subjectivity in the virtual space between subjects, just as music lives in the human musical space. That is also why I prefer in clinical seminars not to have a written text for me to follow; I find that for me this objectifies the analytic relationship too much and I lose the elusiveness of the flow of words that searches for meaning and that I try to listen to.

Finally, in the most recent book *The Evil Imagination (2023)*, it is suggested that what links many evil acts is dehumanizing cruelty associated with the annihilation of the human subject, where human otherness and agency are psychologically denied and/or physically eliminated. At such times, the human subject becomes invaded by the other, subject relations are cancelled, and there is a denial or destruction of the gift of otherness with the carrying out of evil acts.

So, in this way of analytic thinking, analysis is very much about two human beings whose subjective experience is difficult to tie down, and yet in their encounter something vital may happen. As I shall explore later, I think that this is the experience that Freud first describes in *The Interpretation of Dreams*, where the analytic subject first comes most clearly into view.

But why am I revisiting subject relations theory and in particular those early publications where I first sketched it out? Probably for a variety of reasons. First, I recently had some time on my hands, then the American relational psychoanalyst Stephen Seligman, who, when he was editor, had published my 1990 papers on subjectivity in Psychoanalytic Dialogues, was visiting the United Kingdom and giving some talks, and as a friend and colleague I also met with him. Then I finally got round to reading a book which was a commentary in Italian of my *Elusive Human Subject* book, and which helpfully summarized and examined a number of ideas raised there and in some later papers.[26]

With regard to why I wrote the book, I would say that at that time I was dissatisfied with some aspects of object relations theory, particularly the notion of 'internal objects,' which seemed a quaint throwback to a now discarded theory of how our minds are made up, as a Cartesian model of the mind, where the latter is a private theatre where we inspect our thoughts and feelings, which reflects or copies the outer world. The main problem with this model, as shown by Wittgenstein and Ryle, for example, is who looks at the internal theatre and who observes the observer? While there are undoubtedly organized elements in our minds, which are evident in our unconscious life as described by Freud in *The Interpretation of Dreams*, there is a deep problem in describing us as having specific internal objects, though this may be how psychotic patients may experience their minds, as literally having physical objects taking them over; Bion described this well. I prefer to retain the term 'objects' for physical objects and 'others' when talking about people and subjects relating to other subjects. Or as Freud put it, '*psychical* reality is not to be confused with *material* reality.'[27]

I also felt at that time that we had lost the importance of what I felt I was doing and seeing, the frailties, paradoxes and struggles of the human subject and the difficulties in capturing these experiences with current psychoanalytic thought. There was also at that time the beginnings of a considerable interest in the psychoanalytic literature on the nature of the human subject. Ogden wrote two review papers on the topic and a book[28] in which he discussed in considerable detail the analytic conception of the subject. The latter is for him, 'the cornerstone of the psychoanalytic project and is at the same time one of the least well-articulated psychoanalytic concepts.'[29]

As I pointed out in the previous chapter, intersubjectivity as a central concept was also being used by, for example, Robert Stolorow and his colleagues,[30] who used it as a framework for a theory of relatedness. For them, Intersubjectivity provides the essential context for relating. They emphasized the mutual and reciprocal interplay of subjective worlds, including that of the analyst, in an intersubjective 'field.' Although I would not disagree with the need to look at the interactive dimension between people, I think that the intersubjective theory they put forward is essentially an interpersonal theory. The nature of the subject is rather loosely defined and owes much to self-psychology; that is the subject in this theory is really a self. The nature of the subject is not really 'well-articulated,' to use Ogden's phrase.

I had also been deeply influenced by the thought of Jacques Lacan, about whom I had co-authored a study in the 1980s. He considered that the psychoanalytic experience runs its course entirely on the relationship of subject to subject, signifying in effect that it retains a dimension which is irreducible to any psychology considered as an objectification of certain properties of the individual.[31] Lacan's complex model of the subject reveals how subjects are formed and transformed by chains and networks of meaning, or in his terms signifiers.

I was also influenced by meetings that the Independent Group had with the Self Psychologists in the 1990s. This meant becoming exposed more intimately to relational psychoanalysis, where intersubjectivity began to become increasingly central in analytic thinking, even if in the end my own version of intersubjectivity was less relational and more Freudian.

Of course, it goes without saying that Independent analytic thinking has been the basis of my approach, with openness to different forms of thought, a pluralistic approach, with the analyst having a multiplicity of analytic voices at their disposal in order to take account of the complexity of the patient's mind and world. This is captured well by Milan Kundera's description of novelistic thinking, which is,

> ...fiercely independent of any system of preconceived ideas; it does not judge; it does not proclaim truths; it questions, it marvels, it plumbs; its form is highly diverse: metaphoric, ironic, hypothetic, hyperbolic, aphoristic, droll, provocative, fanciful; and mainly it never leaves the magic circle of its characters' lives.[32]

I would add that in addition the analyst needs to attend to the concrete realities of daily life.

Winnicott's thinking was also central to the 1998 book, not only the importance of a transitional space in child development, but also his notion of how the patient can come to 'use' the analyst. In his paper 'The use of an object,'[33] he first describes 'object-relating,' which refers to when the subject is an isolate, who is then functioning at an omnipotent level. A more mature level of functioning occurs when the subject can use an object (i.e., another person). The change from object relating to using involves a process where the subject in fantasy destroys the other but the other survives the destruction. The subject then enters a world where others are available for use in this positive sense, and the subject can have live contact with others. This for me is the earliest description of the patient 'becoming a subject' in analysis.

The Dream Subject

Having decided to revisit my early work, I thought I would go back to the beginning when the Freudian subject was first being described in detail, that is, *The Interpretation of Dreams*.

'It is my experience, and one to which I have found no exception, that every dream deals with the dreamer himself [die Eigene Person].'[34] In *The Interpretation of Dreams*, Freud himself is the subject of many of the dreams, as they offered, '...a copious and convenient material, derived from an approximately normal person and related to multifarious occasions of daily life.'[35] What Freud describes time and again is how a dilemma from fragments of daily life, or what I have called the 'Work of the day,'[36] gets carried over into the dream, links with early psychical material such as a childhood or infantile wish, and is worked into a scenario for the dreaming subject to experience. The unconscious weaves [umspinnt] its connections round apparently indifferent or even rejected preconscious impressions and ideas.[37] 'Unconscious scenes'[38] exercise an attraction on the forces producing the dream work, forcing themselves into perception, however disguised by, for example, condensation and displacement.

In the long dream analysis of a pivotal specimen dream, that where his patient Irma appeared, we have displayed the twists and turns of Freud's subjective life, through a range of transformations, with the presentation of different images and themes from his life. Freud as subject of the dream appears and disappears through different figures, different subjective positions as the unconscious chain weaves its way.

Irma was a hysterical patient who in treatment was relieved of her hysterical anxiety but retained some somatic symptoms. In a summer vacation, Freud met his friend Otto who knew the patient, and when Freud asked him how she was doing, Otto replied that she was better but not quite well, in a way that Freud felt indicated a reproof that he was critical of Freud and sided with Irma's family who were always against the treatment. That night Freud wrote out her case history with the idea of giving it to Dr M, a common friend, in order to justify himself.

That night, he had the long *Irma dream*, in which, in summary, she appears among numerous guests in a big hall. Taking her to one side near a window Freud tries to justify himself that if she still has pains, it was her fault. But when he looked at her, she appeared pale and puffy, and he was alarmed that he had missed something organic. He looked into her mouth and saw a big white patch and scabs on the features, which looked like nasal bones. He called in Dr M, who looked different from usual with a limp, and Otto was there, and another friend, Leopold, who was examining her and found organic disease. They all became aware of the origin of the infection – Otto had given her an injection of trimethylamine (a substance linked through Freud's associations to the chemistry of sexual processes) with a probably dirty syringe.

The day's residues were clear, concerning the news that Otto had brought about Irma's condition, and Freud's feeling of being criticized, which led to his writing out the case history as a justification of his approach. In his analysis of the dream, he uncovered many links between the figures in the dream and other figures in his life. Behind Irma, for example, were two other female patients who were recalcitrant to treatment. The scabs reminded him of his own health when he had taken cocaine, and that led to an association with a patient of his who had developed a necrosis of the mucous membrane of the nose following cocaine use. There was also the link to the Cocaine episode where a close friend had become addicted to cocaine that Freud had been using and recommending as an eye anaesthetic as well as for health and well-being, and that friend had died. Dr M reminded Freud of a patient he had made very ill with prescribing what at that time was a harmless remedy; Freud had turned to Dr M, a senior colleague, for help. Behind Dr M was the figure of Freud's elder brother, who had developed a limp. There were also associations concerning anxiety about his wife's health.

Freud describes how the dream acquitted him of the responsibility of Irma's condition by showing that it was due to other factors, producing a whole series of reasons. He collected many of the themes and ideas that came out of his dream analysis to a 'concern about my own and other people's health – professional conscientiousness.'[39] The dream represented a particular state of affairs as he should have wished to be, with him no longer responsible for a failed treatment and the *wish* to be innocent of Irma's somatic illness; this is the *subjective theme* of the dream, representing a crisis in Freud's professional life and standing, an attack on his professional competence, and a paper-thin attempt to bolster his self-esteem. Yes, the dream represents, and creates, the fulfilment of a wish, but it is a wish concerning the state of the subject's life. In terms more familiar to French psychoanalysis, the dream represents the subject's *desire*.

It took enormous courage for Freud to be so open in public about his underlying anxieties.

Freud's dream of the *Botanical Monograph* which he dreamt he had written,[40] also led to dream thoughts concerned with the complications and conflicts arising between colleagues from their professional obligations and also the self-reproach that he sacrificed too much for the sake of his hobbies. He had seen a plant monograph in the window of a book shop the day before, and his associations led once again to the Cocaine episode. The words botanical and monograph led in turn to a whole stream of associations, including exams in botany from school and university and the excessive cost of his hobbies. The words botanical and monograph were described as 'nodal points' [Knotenpunkten], upon which a great number of the dream thoughts converged, leading to his crucial concept of overdetermination, where each of the elements of the dream is represented in the dream thoughts many times over.

Much of the dream book then concerns the structure of the dream and what leads to its particular form. On the one hand, the dream is not made to be understood, and is mysterious, enigmatic; it ultimately reaches into the unknown, the 'navel of the dream'[41] On the other hand, essential dream thoughts emerge as a complex of memories and thoughts of the most intricate structure with more than one centre of focus or theme, with multiple centres of activity and with some ready-made structures such as organized phantasies being available for being dragged into the dream construction.[42]

While much of what I have outlined is familiar, I would like to emphasize how we can see here how Freud is creating the psychoanalytic subject; behind all the various dream figures, Freud the dreamer weaves his way in a psychic journey through his past and present anxieties, in a dream language he has deciphered and which he describes throughout the book. Through the shifting in and out of different characters and situations, Freud reveals different aspects of himself, 'die Eigene Person' or subject. The analytic subject emerges for the first time. The subject of a person's dream is indeed the human subject, the subject's theme and variations, what I try to listen for in an analytic session. One could call this paying attention to the 'state of the subject.' It's a kind of 'decentred' listening, paying attention not just to what underlies communications but what seems 'off centre.' Dreams, one might say, are not just to be deciphered; they are not the only 'royal road to a knowledge of the unconscious activities of the mind,'[43] but also the means of being in touch with the patient's different subjective positions or states of mind.

One could see that there is a kind of parallel between the shifting in and out of different characters as in the Irma dream, and the way that the subject in waking life also goes in and out of different states of mind as they weave their way through different interactions with other subjects.

The changes in subjective states imply the existence of multiple positions that the subject can occupy and many ways in which the subjective organization can be put together. Pathological organizations are structured rigidly around a central theme, which could be a trauma, a delusion, or a bodily preoccupation.

The process of Freud's dream interpretation also reveals the elusiveness of our subjective lives, the 'inner shadowy and unknown zone,' described by Roussillon. The dream reveals truths about us, however disguised in dream language, and yet the dream remains fleeting, elusive, here and then gone, with maybe just some fragments remaining in conscious memory. But in the analytic encounter, the dream thoughts, brought to life through the processes of free association and analytic reverie, can piece together the dream's meanings. The subject's elusive truth can be found, or recreated, if only through the unweaving of fragments of associations; the analyst's listening activity provides a framework for the elucidation of the dream thoughts. This of course is the basis for other aspects of the psychoanalytic encounter, not just dream interpretation; analytic listening allows the patient's 'voice' to emerge.

The human subject is located in two different spaces, localities or 'scenes,' the elusive dream space and the tangible social space of everyday life. Perhaps what ties them together is the human imagination, the unifying principle active not only in the dream, which Freud calls the process of combining into a unity [Einheit],[44] but also in the synthetic function of the creative imagination in daily life.

Analysts start with the patient's dream and hope to reach the network of dream thoughts which instigated the dream; poets start with the dream thoughts and through their creative imagination create a 'dream.'

Clinical Issues

My own clinical approach is quite straightforward and begins with the technique Freud describes in *The Interpretation of Dreams*, getting to the subject's anxieties and issues through listening to their associations. As the dream is the conjunction of sources from daily life, or Freud's 'multifarious occasions of daily life,' conjoined to an unconscious theme from infancy or childhood, I listen from the beginning to the patient's history, and how that comes into the clinical presentation and the everyday work of the analysis, listening to both the history of layers and the history of events. I think that there are different ways to access the patient's subjective life – through gradual interpretation, specific attention to dream life, contact with the analyst's human aspects, which I have described in *The Elusive Human Subject*, where I gave several clinical examples as illustrations, as well as specific interpretation of the transference.

The 2000 paper Becoming a Subject describes what I still think is relevant clinically. An analyst starts in an analytic session waiting for something to emerge. What will emerge one hopes will be uncertain, surprising, or something that can spark some of one's own associations. The analyst wants to see what will come out of the patient's narrative. From time to time the analyst may be able to nudge the patient's narrative, where appropriate and in the interests of the treatment, offering some kind of 'punctuation' of the narrative. Other times, the patient will follow associations, sometimes leading to something surprising, other times down a blind alley. Breakdowns of communication, failures in understanding can become either impasses or possibilities for change. I have described these kinds of moments in various papers, such as one involving the analysis of a troubled adolescent,[45] and in the analysis of an adult who was sexually abused as a child.[46] The hope is that eventually, however long it takes, and it usually does take a long time, the patient will find their own voice, which is what I would describe as *becoming a subject*, owner of their various experiences and of their own life.

What I mean by this is that the patient brings to us all sorts of different stories, fixed patterns of relating or symptoms, hopes, expectations, and resistances. Patients often come with a sense of isolation; of either being alone with suffering or suffering from being alone. And they come to analysis, subject to various forces in their life, past and present. If the analysis works, then there is the possibility of their becoming the subject of their experiences and ultimately of their lives, with a sense of being no longer isolated and more in contact with others. Becoming a subject, then, involves a shift towards a subjective position. What I mean by this is that the term subjective position involves some capacity to take up different positions without their becoming fixed in a kind of frozen state of being. Being the subject of actions and thoughts is different from being subject to them or being in an 'objective position' where actions and thoughts and so on are not felt to be part of the subject's life. In order to be fully in touch with another person, in a truly subjective position, one begins to grasp the other's point of view; the other is seen as other, a person or a subject, in a context, orientated to others and being affected by others in the social world. A subjective position involves allowing experiences of the other, at many levels, conscious and unconscious, to interpenetrate oneself, so that they make an impact.

In the analytic encounter, the analyst may have to bear being in a number of different subjective positions in the session, rather than allowing himself to become fixed in one place, although at any moment he may find himself 'moored' in one place more favoured than another. I would suggest that the analyst's free-floating attention consists in a subjective oscillation between different positions or moorings. This means having to tolerate a considerable amount of ambiguity, uncertainty, and paradox. This situation involves difficulties for patients for whom uncertainty is very difficult to tolerate.

For example, they may find the analyst's openness to the unconscious both a challenge and, at times, confusing.

In any shift towards a subjective position, or in becoming a subject, there is often a simultaneous move towards an objective position. That is, when we try to encounter the other fully as subject, we are often taken away to the other as mere object, i.e., with little sense of otherness, and we are constantly shifting between these two positions. In the patient I described in the 2000 and also in the previous chapter, there was a fundamental difficulty in allowing experiences of the other to make an impact. Her body was often used to deflect away from experiencing the other and became almost objectified.

Freud in his papers on technique makes the crucial point in the handling of dream interpretation, but also interpretation in general, that the appropriate analytic stance is to give up conscious purposive aims and be *guided by the unconscious* in establishing links.[47]

Analysts vary greatly on the interpretation of what Freud means here. I also think that analysts vary greatly in how they can read unconscious communications in their patients and in themselves. Experience of doing many years of analysis does help, particularly experience of undertaking intensive analysis rather than less intense psychotherapy.

The French style of psychoanalysis is very much towards interpretations which directly pick up and name unconscious themes, though, for example, a verbal allusion, a play of irony, or just a judicious comment.

An example from a French analyst Laurent Danon-Boileau[48]: A patient arrives for his session saying that that morning, while coming to his session, for some reason he had the thought, 'I want to stop my analysis.' Then after a silence and various comments the patient said that before the session, he had seen a mother crossing a square with her child, visibly pregnant. At that point the patient recalled the moment when his mother had announced that she was expecting a new baby, a little girl. After a silence, the analyst said 'Stop the analysis? So you don't have to hear me tell you that you are going to have a baby sister?' The patient laughed and then produced a dream.

The analyst's interpretation here was first placing themselves in the position of the patient – 'Stop the analysis?' but also questioning the symptom of wanting to stop analysis. Then the analyst places himself in the transference position, of the pregnant mother, and through the interpretation tries to stand in the way of the neurotic repetition, helping the patient to face the mourning of his mother's exclusive love for him.

One can see how in the last example, when the patient is confronted with the dawning of the awareness of their own sibling rivalry, which they will need to own, rather than run away by ending the analysis, a sense of *emerging subjectivity* arises.

From time to time the analyst may be able to nudge the patient on either through comments, or more organized transference interpretations (I try to do both). They will move from what I have called being subject 'to' their history to being subject 'of' their history, that is more active agents. Or they will move in such a way that they will find that, as Aldous Huxley put it, 'Experience is not what happens to you; it is what you do with what happens.'

The analytic space provides a structure, a setting in which the indefinable can become definable, what one could call a *home for the unconscious*.

But for free association to happen, the analytic space needs to be welcoming. Not free from conflict, not always comfortable, of course, but welcoming the unconscious. These precious moments when the analysis may feel more alive may be most intense at various *crossroads* between the processes of coming and going, presence and absence, the past and the present, life and death; along paths taken and glimpses of paths not taken. Some patients seem to live, like one of Pirandello's characters, on the threshold of life, near to living but never quite becoming subjectively alive.

Notes

 1 Nagel (1986, p. 38).
 2 Malcolm (1986, pp.100–101).
 3 Montaigne (2003, p. 740).
 4 Kennedy (1996a).
 5 Kennedy (1997).
 6 Kennedy (1998).
 7 Kennedy (2000).
 8 Bollas (1989, pp. 108–109).
 9 Ehrlich (2003, p. 244).
10 Scruton (2014, p. 72).
11 Rousillon (1999, p. 542).
12 Weinrib (2012).
13 Ogden (1994, p. 25).
14 Kundera (1984).
15 Kennedy (2002, p. 18).
16 Kennedy (2002, p. 50).
17 Freud (1900, p. 603).
18 Freud (1900, p. 525).
19 Wolf (1988, p. 38).
20 Mitchell (1991, p. 124).
21 Mitchell (1991, p. 139).
22 Mitchell (1991, p. 139).
23 Bromberg (1993, p. 166).
24 Kennedy (2014, p. 81).
25 Scruton (2014, p. 147).
26 Bianchetti (2017).
27 Freud (1900, p. 620).
28 Ogden (1992a, 1992b, 1994).
29 Ogden (1992a, p. 624).
30 Stolorow et al. (1994).
31 Benvenuto and Kennedy (1986, p. 101).
32 Kundera (2005, p. 71).
33 Winnicott (1971, pp. 86–94).
34 Freud (1900, p. 322).
35 Freud (1900, p. 105).
36 Kennedy (2007, p. 246ff).

37 Freud (1900, p. 563).
38 Freud (1900, p. 576).
39 Freud (1900, p. 129).
40 Freud (1900, p. 282ff).
41 Freud (1900, p. 525).
42 Freud (1900, p. 590).
43 Freud (1900, p. 608).
44 Freud (1900, p. 228).
45 Kennedy (1990).
46 Kennedy (1996b).
47 Freud (1911, p. 94).
48 Danon-Boileau (2016, pp. 28–29).

4 Presence and Absence in Early Experience

The terms absence and presence describe fundamental states of being. For this reason, they are difficult to define without referring to each other. There is always a play of presence and absence, the visible and the invisible, coming and going, leaving and returning. The *Oxford English Dictionary* definitions of both terms are self-referential: presence is, 'the fact or condition of being present,' and absence is, 'the state of being absent or away.' Both these terms are thus dependent upon the notion of *being*. The OED cites the primary definition of being as 'to have or occupy a place … somewhere.' So being exists within a fundamental framework or 'home' state, from which one may be absent or to which one may return.

Such a basic state of being may help to account for the powerful emotional effect of movements in *music* to and from a tonal centre, when we hear movements away from and back to a *home* key, in a kind of musical 'journey.' Daniel Barenboim[1] describes the 'psychology of tonality,' which parallels the inner life. This is

> creating a sense of home, going to an unknown territory, then returning. This is a process of courage and inevitability. There is the affirmation of the key – you want to call it the affirmation of self, the comfort of the known territory – in order to be able to go somewhere totally unknown and have the courage to get lost and then, find again this famous dominant, in an unexpected way, that leads us back home.

It may account for the uncanny experience of listening to music such as the prelude to Wagner's *Tristan and Isolde*, where the chromatic tonality remains ambiguous. A diminished seventh chord hovers over the music capable of several different resolutions; we don't know whether it will reach home base, creating an intense emotional experience, which no doubt is intended to set the scene for the opera's trajectory of unfulfilled human desire and its deathly transformations.

There are some modern writers where absence is more powerfully alive than presence. Emblematic of this kind of author and of the modernist tone is the work of Franz Kafka. Kafka is haunted by absence – absent powers,

DOI: 10.4324/9781003683315-4

unseen authorities; doors, windows, and stairs that lead nowhere, a veritable architecture of absence. It is as if leaving Plato's dark cave of shadows only leads to another cave of shadows, beyond a wall, another wall. Others may be present beyond the wall, but there is no guarantee, and just as likely to be nothing. *Other presences* are lacking.

These are also issues that get played out in psychoanalysis. Many of our patients come to us without much sense of being themselves, or not having a sense of their own identity, or a place or home where they feel secure. With the neurotic patient, there is in the transference a regular kind of coming and going; the analyst is both present and absent for the patient, appears and disappears. Such transference movements do not create massive anxiety or a great deal of loneliness. However, traumatized and borderline patients bring in an intense way the issue of a going away which feels at times total, with no hope of a return and a traumatic sense of loneliness, a Kafka-like landscape of absence. The hope is that the analytic setting can provide some resolution to their despair.

Early experiences can help to understand the psychic situation in adult patients. The neurotic with secure early attachments can stand absence without loss of the sense of self. The borderline patient, with often insecure early attachments, goes in and out of states of unthinkable anxiety, but there is still some sense of a return of the absent object. But with the psychotic patient there is no return, and a sense of utter desolation and emptiness remains.

One could describe the presence/absence dynamic as a pivotal organizing framework, around which one can understand fundamental developmental processes and the way that the early parent manages their own comings and goings with their children.

For convenience, I have divided up the relevant clinical issues into three headings – holding over time, types of absence, and different kinds of mental space.

Holding Over Time

Earlier experiences of separation will, of course, be crucial to how the child manages the waiting time. Winnicott[2] describes how the inner representation of the mother is kept alive in the baby by the reinforcement given from the mother and her technique of devoted childcare. The baby may be distressed by the mother's absence, but if she returns within a reasonable time, this distress is soon mended. Trauma implies that the baby has experienced a break in life's continuity, so that primitive defences come into place to defend against the repetition of unbearable, or unthinkable, anxiety, with attendant confusion and disintegration of ego structure.

Winnicott[3] also describes how the young child can deal with environmental disturbances such as the mother's absence when there is active adaptation to the child's needs. The child can then be in a state of undisturbed isolation. In this state, he can make a spontaneous movement, and the environment is discovered without any loss of the sense of self. There is a respect for processes, a sense of continuity: one experience will follow another; when something occurs in the environment, there is an appropriate reaction. Thus, going away is followed by a return. The child can build up memories of a mother who is both actively present and returns when absent; the situation is *held over time;* there is a secure home base.

But when there has been a failure of good-enough adaptation, with environmental impingement, the child returns to a state of restless isolation. The absence produces no return, or there is such a long wait for the return that there is a loss of the sense of self; the child is in a state of solitary and anxious waiting. In extreme cases, with persistent and repeated absences, this situation may lead to various primitive states of mind, where, instead of the persistence of an internal image of the mother, there is merely a gap, an absence of representation. The gap itself takes possession of the mind, erasing the representations of the object that preceded its absence.

Winnicott also draws attention to the importance for the young baby of dropping things, a precursor, one might say, of the more organized presence/absence experience. The stage of the baby playing at dropping things is seen as a crucial stage around the time of weaning, when there is the beginning of the capacity to master loss. For constructive play to be possible, the loved person needs to have been near the baby in the first place, in order to survive the baby's various anxieties and projections, as well as offer holding over time through their adaptive responses and their safe return.

In fact, Winnicott noted[4] that Freud's fort/da observation, described in *Beyond the Pleasure Principle,*[5] that of his 18-month-old grandson drawing a cotton reel in and out of his cot as his mother came and went, stimulated him to make detailed observations of infants' play between about five and thirteen months of age.

In a paper on the observation of infants in a 'set situation,' he describes a way to observe infants and diagnose some of their difficulties by presenting them, while their mother is present, with a shiny tongue depressor, or spatula. There are usually three possible stages to be observed, corresponding to processes in time of incorporation, retention, and riddance.

In the *first stage*, the child begins, tentatively, to show a spontaneous interest in the spatula. In the *second stage*, after a period of hesitation, the child accepts the reality of the spatula and soon puts it in his mouth. He or she now feels the spatula is in their possession and may bang it on the table or hold it to the observer's mouth, playing at feeding. In *the third stage*, which Winnicott links with the fort/da game, the baby drops the spatula less by mistake than on purpose and thoroughly enjoys aggressively getting rid of it. The end of this phase, when the child is mastering his feelings about the mother's departure, comes when the baby either wishes to get down on the floor with the spatula, where he starts mouthing it and playing with it again, or else when he is bored with it and reaches out to any other objects that lie at hand.

The game of riddance of the object reassures the child about the fate of the internal mother, that she has not vanished, that her image is still alive, and that she is going to return to play with the child again. There is thus a need for the child to be able to throw the mother away symbolically to keep her alive. But of course, this presupposes that the successful negotiation of the earlier phases of incorporation and retention has taken place, so that there is a sense of continuity over time.

Those patients who have had such an experience of continuity are more able to do psychic work; there is an adequate level of symbolic functioning; what goes away can return; they can cope with being on their own. However, in those patients with disruptions in the early holding environment, there may be a retreat from the reality of the social world into a private time, or into a state of almost psychotic timelessness; there is little hope that what goes away can ever return, so it is better to create a state of timelessness, where comings and goings are irrelevant.

With some traumatized and often abused patients, there are also pathological states in which lived time is avoided by a whirlwind of activity, and they may experience rapid changes between extremes in their mental state. The whirlwind of confusion, with so many comings and goings that it is impossible to register any coherent pattern, may be both a defence against experiencing chaos, and a way of re-creating an excited mental state. They may need the whirlwind in order to feel alive, as they have not had the sense of time kept going by the mother.

Different Kinds of Absence

The quality of the contact between mother and child is crucial to how the child will deal with her absence. There are several different kinds of absence. Green's dead mother complex refers to a pervasive and catastrophic absence, with a bereaved and preoccupied mother unable to be alive to the child. There is a void, an emptiness, between mother and child, which leads to a loss of meaning and desperate attempts to patch the hole between them. The shadow of her absence, even when physically present, pervades the child and the analytic patient. This results in a fundamental fantasy: to nourish the dead mother and maintain her perpetually embalmed. She is never 'thrown away' symbolically. When the dead mother complex is touched in the transference, 'the subject feels himself to be empty, blank, as though he were deprived of a stop-gap object and a guard against madness.'[6]

There is a difficult task for the patient, who eventually has to mourn the dead mother rather than keep her embalmed: that of letting her go, getting rid of rather than holding onto her. This task means having to face intense feelings of emptiness, for she has filled the patient's psychic life as a dead presence. Letting her go, that is, bringing to her life and then mourning her loss, means having to face the paradoxical situation of two losses: presence in death and absence in life.

Other patients may not have the dead mother complex, but the quality of the mother's absence may also be an intense issue. For example, in the more psychotic end of the spectrum, there is the non-presence of the object; a void, a nothingness, an emptiness, and blankness. Even if the object returns, it is not enough to heal the disastrous consequences of its too-long absence. The nothingness of this experience is eloquent, communicating a sense of disaster. As one approaches this area in the patient, there may be a futile absence, which may be experienced by the analyst as depression and brought by the patient through enactments. This entails the intense presence of a sense of nothingness, a non-existent or cancelled subject, with little sense of human agency. The hope is that analytic work can provide a framework for the linking of presence to absence, and with it the possibility of becoming a subject.

Bion makes a distinction between nothing and no-thing. Knowledge of loss, of the thought as a no-thing, with a realization of the absent object, can lead to freedom; or else, the patient may be unable to tolerate frustration, and the no-thing may be used as the foundation for hallucination.[7] Green calls the latter negative hallucination and he cites the female patient who said to Winnicott that the negative of him was more real than the positive of him. Parsons also develops this theme when he distinguishes between a constructive and a destructive role for negativity in psychic life. The constructive role of the negative requires a certain psychic mobility, a capacity to shift between negating and affirming, separation and connection.[8] One may see this shift between presence and absence in the pattern of the patient's movements of engagement and disengagement in the transference relationship.

I have described[9] what I called the 'dual aspect' of the transference, which refers to the analyst as simultaneously the receiver of the patient's projections, or the analyst as fantasy object, and as different from these projections. This dual aspect of the transference refers to the way that the more neurotic patient can oscillate from being identical, in the patient's eyes, to archaic fantasies, and being something else, different. I described how to begin with the patient revealed a repetitive transference pattern, in which some analytic work was possible but was then thrown away, so that looking back at what had happened one seemed to be left with a series of fragmented weeks and months. But this was not a helpful throwing away, in that nothing came back, and she was left with a feeling of futility. However, after a considerable amount of work, the transference began to have a more dynamic and less rigid feel. I became less merged with her primitive fantasies, and she was able to see me both as a fantasy figure and as different. This coincided with an ability to hold onto analytic work, rather than merely throw it away.

One is reminded of Winnicott's observation of a boy's use of string as a means both to communicate and to deny separation.[10] The mother of this seven-year-old was a depressive, who had been hospitalized for depression. As a result, there were several extended occasions when the child was separated from the mother. He developed several symptoms, including compulsions and retention of faeces. When he was seen for a consultation, he showed a preoccupation with string; at home he would join up the furniture with string, and had also tied string round his younger sister's neck. The function of the string was seen as a way of trying to communicate the child's fear of separation, by desperately joining up objects. It was as if he were trying to 'rope her in.' It was not just the mother's going away which was traumatic for the child, but also her lack of contact with him when she returned, due to her preoccupation with herself and other matters, her lack of focus on the child. The string both communicated his wish to join up objects and his denial of a painful separation, with an anxious form of attachment. The string was a positive materialization of an absent, negative bond.

One can see a variety of disorganized attachments with those children who have been subjected not just to emotional detachment but also to physical and/or sexual abuse. From my own experience of working with such children and their families, the children are often haunted by their abuse and unable, without considerable help, to flee themselves from its consequences. They often cannot concentrate on a task for long, as if there has been a massive disruption in their capacity to link experiences over time. They appear over-stimulated with poor impulse control and they may have a haunted, driven quality to their relating and a tendency to be aggressive and testing of boundaries. Sometimes they may show inappropriate sexual behaviour; they may go in and out of confusional states when they become very anxious, particularly about being abandoned, and they have great difficulty in trusting adults. The parent-child relationships are usually pathological, with varying degrees of disorganized attachment patterns. There is often role reversal, in which the child tries to control the parents' comings and goings, while the parents have problems in maintaining ordinary child-adult boundaries. These parents often have difficulty in being emotionally attached to their children, with inhibition of the capacity to play. In the child, and probably also in the parent, there is a loss of or failure to develop the capacity to use meaningful symbols; so that as it were, no presence/absence interchange is possible. The parents are often inconsistent, at times cut off, and self-absorbed. The children themselves seem to make a particular kind of powerful emotional impact on their parents and other caretakers, as if they are desperately trying to get the parents to acknowledge their needs and accept the trauma that they have experienced. This may lead to various kinds of anti-social behaviour.

My own experience of the abused adult is that they can recreate the emotionally absent parent at some point. This is the parent who could not bear the child's pain and vulnerability and who has left the child with a sense that the environment has fundamentally failed them and that there is a kind of breach, or unbearable gap, in the parenting experience. An unbridgeable gap may suddenly appear between patient and analyst, which either party may be tempted to deal with by some kind of precipitous action, such as termination. Bearing unbearable emotional pain is an issue in any analysis, but with the abused adult it becomes acutely relevant.

Different Kinds of Mental Space

One may ask what happens to the child between the mother's coming and going. Of course, the effect of prolonged separations on the child is well documented in the attachment literature. Anxiety, ultimately leading to despair and depression, has long been known to occur with, for example, hospitalized children left without a caretaker. Such situations, though originally described by the Robertsons in the 1950s, are, unfortunately, still common throughout the world because of war and famine or poor services for abandoned children left unattended in institutions. The space between the child and the mother will become so vast as to be un-representable. No cotton reel play or its equivalent can ever bring the mother back, and the play is soon abandoned, leaving the child in a despairing and depressed listlessness.

Anxiety about the mother's return and the state when she returns may become organized in the adult patient through perverse functioning, when, for example, there is an attempt to control the other. For example, a narcissistic man came into analysis as he was having difficulty sustaining relationships. He showed little empathy for others and was exploitative and often emotionally sadistic. He sought my admiration to boost his fragile sense of self-worth, while he was dismissive about my capacities. I was treated like a servant, there to attend to his needs. Women were seen as mere objects to be entered. He would gain pleasure from teasing them, keeping them waiting, stirring them up with desire, and then dropping them. However, he also at times after some analysis, experienced an increasing sense of futility about his lifestyle, with how much he needed to fill himself up with sexual excitement and destructiveness in order to avoid feeling empty. What soon became clearer was an all-pervading fear of psychical collapse and a terror of being submerged by me in the transference. The picture of his mother was of a cold, puritanical and panicky figure, brittle and unresponsive. He was left with her when his father was often away from home, and she turned to him for comfort. She became depressed and he felt he had to bolster her up, a situation which he greatly resented. His sadistic use of women could clearly be related to this early mother/child interaction, in which there was an excessive turning to the child for comfort, intrusion into his psychic space, and a fusion of her needs with his.

Effective use of the transitional space clearly represents a more satisfactory way of dealing with the mother/child relationship, based on 'good-enough' environmental provision rather than excessive anxiety and retreat from active engagement. One has a sense of the playful interaction between mother and child, which can both allow her to come and go without excessive anxiety but also allows the child to play alone in her presence and without her intruding.

However, there are anxious situations, repeated in an analysis of, for example, borderline patients, where there is an issue about the space between coming and going when the subject may feel they can never find their way back to the maternal object. Instead, they may feel lost in the space between coming and going. There is little prospect of becoming a subject as there is little hope of re-finding the object.

In Freud's original observation, one can see the fort/da game as a positive use of repetition. The game helped the child to cope with the mother's comings and goings by providing a kind of symbol of her journeys, however primitive. In the space between these comings and goings, the child was able to find a place to play; there was a space for representation. The child could let go of the mother once he had found a repetitive but symbolic means of representing her leaving him. This positive use of repetition contrasts with a more compulsive and insistent quality of repetition described in *Beyond the Pleasure Principle*, which has a more mindless, or 'daemonic,' quality, related to the power of the unconscious repressed. One could imagine a delicate balance between these two kinds of repetition, depending on the time for waiting for the mother's return, what state she was in when she left, what state the child was in when she left, and what state both are in on her return.

Of course, the fort/da game occurs without the mother, and yet there are many occasions when something similar takes place in the presence of the mother. Various kinds of comings and goings occur in the complex interactions between mother and child. The mirroring role between mother and child is of particular significance in this context. For Lacan, the mirror stage plays a pivotal role in his theory as a moment of alienation preceding the fort/da moment of entering the symbolic order. The child sees himself as a whole in the mirror, but it is as an imaginary unity that he sees himself. This contrasts with the reality of his helplessness and his lack of bodily mastery. For Lacan, the formation of the ego begins at this point of alienation in the mirror, with the fascination with one's own image.[11]

Clearly this view of the place of the mirror image is quite different from that of Winnicott and subsequent child and infant researchers, who focus on the role of parental mirroring as structuring the child's affects. For Winnicott,[12] how the mother looks at the baby, and what the baby sees when he looks at the mother, are crucial to the development of the child's sense of self. The mother has a fundamental role here in giving back to the baby the baby's own self. If, for example, the mother's face is unresponsive, then a mirror is a thing to be looked at but not to be looked into. There is, then, no depth to the mother's mirroring role; the child may be left puzzled about what the other's look may bring; they may be left without much experience of ever getting back what they give. With the mirroring and responsive mother, there is a constant process of flexible interchange between her and the baby, so that a kind of primitive game of presence and absence is already taking place between mother and child, but with her present. If she is unresponsive, then she becomes emotionally absent while present, a traumatic situation for the baby.

…

The task of the developing child, as well as that of the adult analytic patient, is, in a sense, to come to the realization that the mother is not a mere physical object, or at least not an object under the child's omnipotent control, but a subject with a mysterious, elusive life of her own, relating to other subjects, the father and others. The dawning of this realization is never easy; there is always a certain amount of strain involved in the process, more so when the mother's absence is prolonged, or her return highly problematic. If the child is full of anxiety about the mother's absence, then there is little space for imagining where she has been and with whom, that is, for having a sense of *other presences*.

Notes

 1 Barenboim and Said (2002, pp. 46–47).
 2 Winnicott (1971, p. 97).
 3 Winnicott (1958, pp. 222–223).
 4 Winnicott (1958, p. 68).
 5 Freud (1920, S.E. 18, pp. 3–64).
 6 Green (1983, p. 162).
 7 Bion (1970, pp. 16–17).
 8 Parsons (2006, p. 185).
 9 Kennedy (1984).
10 Winnicott (1971, pp. 15–20).
11 Benvenuto and Kennedy (1986, p. 55ff).
12 Winnicott (1971, p. 111ff).

5 What are Fathers for?

When thinking about this topic, I started by putting down a few random impressions about fathering, mainly from my own experience as a father and from watching other fathers, I thought I would share these impressions before presenting anything coherent.

What are fathers for? – They play football with the children, or they're supposed to. Or, anyway, they're meant to rescue the ball when it's unreachable, regardless of the stinging nettles. They go to football matches and mingle with the other blokes. They repair the lock on the back door; well, they've been promising to do it but have never quite managed. Fathers promise a lot… Fathers are meant to be there, I think I am in fact; but I have noticed many are not, though they imagine they are. I notice X. coming home, late as usual, after a day at the office, or has he been somewhere else? With a nag like his wife, I don't blame him. I'm being bigoted or, anyway, uncharitable. Maybe he makes her nag… Fathers step in – to do things, punish, and play. But what do they step into? Is it a trap, chaos, or what? They lay down the law. But does anyone take any notice? Dads take little boys to the men's loo when they are of a certain age, when they're 'big enough.'

> He overeats, doesn't know when to stop. He's the dustbin…Don't talk to your mother like that! Dad! Dad! Don't disturb your father…He never washes up, he always comes home tired. I'm worried about him, he overeats, and smokes too much. He's working too much. He'll have a heart attack soon, and then where will we be?

You may have noticed how anxiety has begun to creep in here. Indeed, it is with considerable trepidation that I approach the topic of fatherhood. Perhaps my work as a psychoanalyst may help me to at least understand the anxiety.

Getting close to your father – it does so often seem to be a difficult issue for fathers and children alike. The French psychoanalyst J-B Pontalis, in his autobiographical book *Love of Beginnings,* has a vivid description of the sort

DOI: 10.4324/9781003683315-5

of tenderness that can arise between fathers and sons, albeit touched with tragedy, as his father died three days later. I quote:

> On the table where I write, before my eyes, there is a photograph. The only one I ever wanted to put in a frame, not so as to preserve it better, for I would have kept it anyway, but, I believe, because it represents precisely what I made for a long while into the frame of my life. Is it necessary to add: the imaginary frame? A father and his son, a man standing next to a child, one hand resting on a shoulder. They're not speaking to each other, they're being photographed. They are looking at the camera. They loyally allow themselves to be captured by the lens that cannot strip them of anything. On the contrary, it's going to represent them, to make them present, together, for all time…This photograph became for me the very image of mutual protection, all the more so as it was taken in a place devastated by war and bears the marks of that: the ruins of a blockhouse, corrugated iron and concrete, a hole, an enormous crater dug by bombs. The son knows that he has a father. The father knows that he has a son. They hold each other. They count on each other. Together they are invulnerable. The hole is not for them.[1]

I thought it best to introduce my account with a question, as there are currently so many doubts about the role and function of fathers in the family. I should say that I am, on the whole, limiting myself to psychological issues and not to issues of a wider sociological kind, though there is obviously some overlap between the fields of psychology and sociology. In addition, I am speaking as a psychoanalyst and much of what I have to say now is based on my experience of treating individuals and families whose lives have either broken down completely, and/or who have suffered considerably. It is my experience that the place, or absence, of their father has often seemed to be of vital importance in understanding the origin and nature of their troubles. Psychoanalysis, both in its theoretical and clinical tasks, is, one might say, a form of 'practical knowledge,' lacking in scientific precision. Its object of knowledge is the human subject seen at close quarters, his or her nature, conflicts and desires. Its theoretical task may, however, conflict with one of its main therapeutic aims, to discover what is in the person's best interests; this may include having to take more account of his or her relationships with others, including partners, children and work colleagues, and may entail producing considerable discomfort in the person undergoing analysis. However, both in its theoretical and clinical senses, one could see psychoanalysis as an ethical activity concerned with the kind of life lived by individuals, most of whom come to the analyst with a crisis of some kind in their mode of living. The analytic encounter is frequently a struggle with the patient's beliefs, interests, and values, a struggle with conflicting viewpoints, the hopeful result of which is that they can come up with a new view of themselves. Perhaps one could demarcate roughly mothering and fathering elements in the analytic encounter. The mothering elements refer to the setting, the kind of care provided by the analyst, the holding function, and the dependency felt by the patient. The fathering elements may refer more to the boundary setting, confrontation, otherness, power and authority issues, and sense of difference. Of course, I am simplifying the situation. Are things as clear as this?

There is an idea that the father's role was clear enough until the modern era. He was important, a V.I.P. As Shakespeare put it, in a Midsummer Night's Dream:

'To you your father should be as a god;
One that composed your beauties yea, and one
To whom you are but as a form in wax
By him imprinted, and within his power
To leave the figure, or disfigure it...
your eyes must with his judgement look.'
(Act 1. scene 1.)

Shakespeare shows how such an attitude only leads to despair and confusion, which results in the mix-up of lovers in the Athenian woods, and, happily, a final resolution. The plays of Molière are also full of the absurdities of fathers who attempt to dictate to their children how they should behave and whom they should marry. Perhaps here one should begin to make a distinction between masculinity and paternal authority. There is the sense of being masculine that comes from close contact with the father; then there is the age-old problem of male authority and the founding and dominating position taken by men and fathers that is full of conflict and social controversy. Shakespeare also reveals the darker side of the father in, for example, King Lear. The tragedy can be understood at many levels, but one level relevant to my theme is that of distorted family relations. Of his three daughters, Cordelia is the absolute favourite. However, he loves her in a monstrously possessive fashion. When it comes to the dividing of his kingdom, he wishes her to put her love for him above all other loves, which of course she cannot do, if she is to become a woman. The sisters, Goneril and Regan, used to being in Cordelia's shadow are now used to hypocrisy, and can pretend their love is exclusive, and Lear does not mind one way or the other. In fact, these sisters, deprived of their father's love and witnesses of his possessive attachment to Cordelia, become hypocritical monsters who ultimately die over their wish to possess the illegitimate Edmund. Edmund himself is deprived of his father's presence. When the play opens, his father the Duke of Gloucester, who will later be blinded, tells how Edmund has to remain distant from his father:

He hath been out nine years. and away he shall again.
(Act 1. scene 1.)

Edmund seeks vengeance by displacing the true-born Edgar. The play, then, seems to revolve around the question of the father's role, and reveals the disastrous consequences when this role is distorted, when, for example, the father is possessive, shows undue favouritism, is absent, or where there is no mother to lessen the father's harsh authority. So perhaps now one could say that we may not know yet what fathers are for, but when they are absent, or when present and they abuse their position, there is profound trouble for those around them.

The absent Father is a fairly common feature of those who come for psychoanalysis, as well as the current experience of considerable numbers of children in the community. Does it matter if there is no father? Of course, it all depends on the circumstances, on the nature of the mother-child relationship, and in particular on the mother's attitude to fathers. There is evidence to show that a child's psychological development can be interfered with if fathers leave the parental home or are largely absent from it. For example, one may see in the children considerable anxieties about the mother: that she might also leave. The young child may feel excessively responsible for the loss and guilt-ridden about having been naughty, fearing that they drove the father away. Such children may also experience problems in adolescence in establishing a masculine or feminine identity. Girls may feel the loss of the father as a confirmation of their inadequate bodies. In the absence of a male model, boys may experience considerable confusion about the mother's position, experiencing her as castrating, overwhelming, or invasive. There is also evidence that the extent and quality of any disturbances in the children are greater the earlier the age at which the loss of the father occurred. However, this kind of data is somewhat biased, in that these are families which, anyway, must have had considerable conflict and marital disharmony, and this in itself might account for at least some of the children's troubles.

I have just referred to the physical absence of the father, but, of course, the situation may be more subtle, in that there may be a psychological absence, even when the father is in the home. The father may opt out of family responsibilities or be allowed to opt out. One can often see this clearly in families in which the mother has suffered a severe mental breakdown after the birth of her baby – so-called 'post-natal depression.' The birth of a baby is ordinarily a time when women are especially vulnerable. Primitive anxieties are stirred up at a time when it is essential to be adult and responsible for a new life. It is usually pleasurable, but for some women and babies this unique and specific developmental stage can be traumatic. One of the main tasks for a new mother is the renegotiation of the mothering which she herself had. If this was good enough, she can tend her baby and fulfil its needs. But if there were severe problems in her own early mothering, this turning back to the grandmother can represent a major threat to the mother's mental health. The turning back can provoke considerable anxiety and confusion. The woman may not be able to differentiate herself from the baby, while she may feel, irrationally, that her own mother disapproves of her. In my past experience of treating such women with their husbands and children living all together at the Cassel Hospital for some months at a time, such problems in the mother can be helped or greatly lessened if the mother is adequately supported by the father. In the absence of such support, the mother is most vulnerable to a major depression. When breakdown then occurs in her, she might quite inappropriately turn to the baby for comfort and protection. Fathers in these families not infrequently tend to view the breakdown as all the mother's fault. They may indeed come across as having tried everything possible to help, and yet, when one looks more closely, there is a subtle attempt to put the vulnerability and disturbance into the woman, with an attempt to extricate themselves from any responsibility for what has happened. In turn, the mother may vociferously defend their husband's right to work all hours at the office and never see their partner and child, as money is needed to keep the family going. Furthermore, when one looks closely, there may be in one or both partners a difficulty in matching up sexual desire and emotional tenderness and comfort. The mother around the time of the birth becomes particularly focused on the baby; she becomes a nursing mother. It may be difficult for her and the father to put together their new roles.

There is also, I believe, the important contribution of the personality of the baby in arousing the parents' responses. Some babies are placid, while others are wakeful, whatever the parents do; some feed well, while others have difficulties. There are no absolute rules about how a baby will turn out. Things can go wrong when the parents cannot be constantly flexible and perceptive about changes in the baby's state of physical and emotional well-being. I am not at all sure how much the capacity to monitor the baby's changing state is a function of the mother or the couple. In fact, I would suggest that one can see the mother and the father as having interrelated and overlapping roles and functions, but with some definite areas of difference, such as when the mother is breastfeeding.

This leads on to the controversial area of who does what, the so-called 'separate spheres' issue, regarding male and female roles and functions. I will return to this issue soon, but before that, I will tackle some of the more difficult clinical issues surrounding child abuse and the role of fathers. In these highly problematic families, one may see how roles are either too rigid or very muddled when fixed and pathological roles are maintained by both partners without questioning.

There are many kinds of families in which abuse takes place. There has usually been a breakdown in parenting functions in many areas of life. To see what happens to fathering in these circumstances, it is impossible to forget the role of the mother. Although these are extreme situations, one may be able to learn something about ordinary fathering when the father's role becomes so disturbed.

One could say that there are three basic situations where child abuse occurs: there is an active male or female abuser, who is the main instigator and perpetrator; there is the complicit abuser or 'inciter,' usually a woman inciting the man; and the denier, also usually a woman, who does not want to believe that her partner has abused their child or children. The denier, as with the others, may also be intimidated by the partner. But I have to say that in my experience of the really difficult cases, intimidation is often fairly mutual, if I can put it like that. I should also say that the male perpetrator does not have to be some obviously violent thug. He is just as likely to be a rather passive and apparently unassuming person, heavily dependent on his partner – what one might call the Violent Wimp. The woman, frequently a denier, often has to prop him up, but then his seething resentment about his partner's power over him may suddenly erupt into violence. The father attacks the child, both because it is the most sadistic way of getting at the woman and because he is so dependent on her. These kinds of fathers are difficult to treat. However, I have often found that the male perpetrator of physical abuse, who has been incited by his partner, may be more emotionally available than his female partner and more able to use therapy. In child abuse cases, it is just as important to look at the quality of mothering as it is the abuse from a perpetrator. Where there is a good enough mothering bond, it is rare to see a father actually harm a child. In many of these families, the paternal-like authority of the law has to take over from the parents, to a greater or lesser extent, where their own authority as parents and their capacity to take responsibility for their children and keep them safe from harm have broken down. These parents are often enormously threatened by the possibility of experiencing in themselves feelings of vulnerability and dependency – the woman just as much, and sometimes more so, than the men. The abused child, at a particular moment of vulnerability, for example, when they show signs of temper and separateness from their parents' control, can be suddenly experienced by the parent as an enormous threat. The psychic pain shown by the helpless or out-of-control child cannot be tolerated by the abusing parent, who then may turn to a sort of extreme paternal attitude of impatience and violent disciplining. In many of the mothers, the relationship to their own fathers has been a violent one, where they have been physically and/or sexually abused. So often in these families, there is the presence not only of the current father and partner, but also of the violent paternal grandfather. With a damaged sense of themselves, these women are at risk of finding similar men to their fathers; and, as workers in this field know only too well, it may be very difficult for them to leave the violence behind – it may become attractive and exciting to them.

To return to the more general issues concerning fathers, there is little doubt that the belief that men and women occupy separate spheres has been used to keep women in an inferior social position. There has been confusion between men and women having different bodies and their being different with regard to their capacities. The fact that women are vulnerable over the short period of childbirth has been used to assert that they are the vulnerable sex, unable to do many jobs, and so on. I would agree with some writers that one of the major reasons for this attitude is the male envy of the woman's capacity to have a baby. However, that is different from going to the opposite extreme and asserting that, as the female has the ability to give birth and nurse the offspring, the male, and hence the father, has nothing at all to give at this time, and that any old helper would be as good as a father. Such an extreme attitude also leaves out the fact that, on the whole, and despite the problems, most men and women actually like to be with each other. In a sense, the whole question about male and female functions is complicated by this rather simple fact: if men and women did not like to live together, then there would be no problem about who does what. I would suggest that the function of the father around the time that the child is an infant consists of the following inter-locking elements: Being part of a couple interested and exquisitely adapted to the baby's needs; offering physical as well as emotional support to the nursing mother; and being different, that is offering another viewpoint to that of the mother, who, particularly in the first months, may be very much bound up with the baby in a very close and physical way. Once the child is growing, the role the father and mother change, in that the mother is their longest so vulnerable to the patterns so preoccupied with the child – then maybe trips to the cinema, and even the occasional dinner party! At this point, one might with justification bring in the importance of how the child identifies with the father, that is the importance of the Oedipus complex. I would just emphasize here. The complicating factor is introduced by the difference with regard to how boys and girls go through the complex – the boy must turn away from the mother as a result of the father's prohibition on incest, but the boy finds another object of the same sex as the mother. While with the girl, she has to turn away from the mother and to find an object of a different sex from the mother. There are, then, fundamentally different developmental tasks for men and women, which must influence their future roles as mothers and fathers.

Since Freud, psychoanalysts have retained the central importance of the Oedipus complex and have also added modifications. For Klein, the father is the 'third' person, through whom the Oedipus complex is initiated. The child turns to the father in order to deal with very primitive fears of destroying or damaging the mother through aggressive fantasies. Thus, turning to the father is a fundamental element of the Oedipus complex. When the father is literally absent, or absent in the mother's mind, then there will be distortions in the child's development, leaving them vulnerable to being submerged by primi-tive fantasies. The significant element for the child his having some notion of a couple. This does not imply that one-parent families are harmful. What seems to matter is how the one parent keeps in mind the notion of the other parent, of otherness and difference.

Jacques Lacan places particular emphasis on the role of the Father. It is, for him, the father's job to enable the child to escape from the intense rela-tionship with the mother. The father is the representative of the 'law' of soci-ety, that is, in this context, the law that incest is prohibited, as well as the law of the language system. The father introduces the principle of law, the epitome of which is the law of language, which the child begins to acquire from a young age. Without the father's law, a person may end up with a serious mental disturbance. The father does not always have to be present for the acquisition of the father's law. He wrote of the essential structure of the 'Name of the Father,' *Le Nom du Pere*. The mother's own relation to her father may be sufficient if the place of the father is valued by her and not denigrated or denied. There may be mental disturbance in a family with a distant father whose messages only come to the child through the mother's mediation, or with a father so besotted with the mother that he cannot function separately and can never provide an alternative to the mother's viewpoint.

To summarize:

I began with the evidence that, in certain circumstances, the loss of a father or his absence, physical and/or psychological, can have a harmful effect on the emotional development of the child. I have emphasized the importance of the father around the birth of a child as part of a couple adapted to the child's needs. I have suggested that an important aspect of the father is his difference. Not only does he provide for good or bad a masculine model, an idea of what it is like to be a man, but he is important in offering or promoting difference. I have also outlined some aspects of the father's functions in the Oedipus complex, where he comes in to prohibit incest with the mother, provides an alternative to the mother, but also becomes part of a couple which the child may feel as united with or against him. It is also possible that the father has a pivotal role in enabling the child to develop symbols and language. This may be first of all as a result of enabling the child to become more separate from the mother. Turning away from the mother to the father is, as it were, the prototype of symbolization, which one could understand as one thing standing for another. It is also possible that the father, or whoever is in the paternal position, by prohibiting incest with the mother, represents a fundamental law of relationships, which in turn forms the structure for symbolization and hence language acquisition.

Having begun with an anxious question about the role of fathers, I seem to have offered some fairly definite answers, although I am certain there are many more aspects to the field than I have been able to cover. I will end with some more uncertainty. Whatever ideas we may have about the father's or the mother's role, it is the child who has to find their way through the maze of our structures and our doubts and hesitations. There is no easy answer to how a person acquires a sense of their own identity. The relation to the mother is the most vital relationship of one's life, in the sense that without a satisfactory bond with her, or her substitute, life itself may not be possible. But it is with the entry of the third person, the father, that the child begins to be aware of its own identity. Until that point, the child has no need really to define themselves, for all is somehow given. And, moreover, the child's deep life-and-death dependency on the mother makes it difficult for it to question its own identity, without, that is, the support of the third person.

Bruno Bettelheim uses the example of Goldilocks and the Three Bears to illustrate these issues in his book *The Uses of Enchantment*.[2] It is an ambiguous tale without a happy or clear ending; rather, it ends with Goldilocks's anxious running away from the Bears. Although there is no resolution in the tale, it does reveal, in symbolic form, some of the essential and painful tasks of growing up.

Goldilocks explores the objects from the three bears – father, mother, and baby, that is the Oedipal threesome. She could be seen as exploring the different identities and positions of the three bears. She first chooses the father's porridge, but it is too hot, and his chair is too hard. Disappointed that intimacy with the father is not possible, she turns back to the mother, but her things are too cold or too soft. Finally, the only thing left to her is to have the baby things, but all is not right there, either, for she has outgrown the baby chair, which she breaks.

When she is woken up by the bears, she runs away as if from a bad dream without finding what really fits her. The story thus illustrates the meaning of the difficult choice the child must make: is he or she to be like father, mother, or child? While the child may be too small to be in their parents' place, simply being in the child's place is in itself no solution. To become oneself, as Bettelheim points out, one has to become something different from either parent or from merely being the child, and that is very difficult.

Notes

1 Pontalis (1986, p. 104).
2 Bettleheim (1976).

6 A Severe Form of Breakdown in Communication in the Psychoanalysis of an Ill Adolescent

Introduction

Five times weekly psychoanalysis of the severely suicidal or psychotic adolescent is difficult and demanding for the patient and the analyst, both of whom require a fair amount of motivation in order to keep going through the many difficult patches. There are bound to be periods in which the patient will feel acutely suicidal, will feel strongly like opting out of the analysis, will make attacks on the setting or will bring profound difficulties in communicating and relating for understanding. The analyst in turn may not infrequently feel tempted to relinquish his or her role, to attempt to *do* something rather than continue to analyze, or may feel hopeless and alone with an unbearable responsibility.

Part of the strain for the analyst may be that there often seems to be an expectation in psychoanalytic treatment that the analyst should always be 'in touch' with the analysand in several different ways. Put simply, one could say that the analyst's 'in-touchness' consists of three interlocking elements – an appropriate physical setting, adequate intellectual understanding, and selective emotional responsiveness. While I am not denying the central importance of being in touch with the patient as far as possible, I think that one can say that there are often moments, particularly in the psychoanalysis of psychotic and borderline psychotic subjects, when there are major breakdowns in communication between analyst and analysand. Such moments are perhaps more sustained and serious in those subjects with whom I am particularly concerned in this paper, who have experienced a major interference in functioning, such as a suicide attempt or a serious psychotic breakdown. In this latter group, the three elements of the analyst's in-touchness may be interfered with, so that the setting may no longer be safe, the analyst's intellectual grasp of the analysis may be severely compromised, and/or their emotional awareness blunted. I wish to suggest that there are times when such breakdowns in communication, which threaten the analyst's in-touchness, are useful, even though at the time of their occurrence they may be distressing, bewildering, and frustrating for both analyst and analysand.

DOI: 10.4324/9781003683315-6

The purpose of this paper is to describe, with clinical material, what I have called for convenience a *core* breakdown in communication, in the ill adolescent. I hope that some of the points I make may also be applicable to the analysis of ill adults. In the discussion I shall distinguish, with references to the literature, this form of breakdown of communication from other, rather less serious, forms of communication problem.

The Core Breakdown in Communication

In this rather loose category, I include those who have experienced a real breakdown in mental functioning, such as a severe suicide attempt or one or more psychotic episodes in which the patient loses touch with the real world or has delusional ideas about themselves, their body, or others. I think that, in this group, a major breakdown in communication is both significant and inevitable at some point in the analysis. It cannot be avoided, however well one analyses, and one could also argue that, unless such difficulties are brought right into the treatment, the patient's pathology will not be significantly shifted. Such a breakdown may be experienced by the analyst in the following way.

Over days, weeks, or even months, there appears to be endless repetition, little sense of the analysis going anywhere, sometimes with unproductive silences, and with a constant strain on the analyst's stamina. A predominant feeling in the analyst, though strangely not always in the patient, is of feeling out of touch, or of having only fleeting moments in touch, with the patient. The sessions appear to be dead, and the analyst does not know what is going on, but it is a most uncomfortable and worrying uncertainty. Dreaming may take place but one begins to doubt its significance and usefulness. The recounting of the dream may itself have an unreal quality, or the patients may be doing all the interpreting themselves, as if they thought they were the analyst; that is, the dream itself and/or the recounting of it to the analyst may disguise a psychotic wish to live in the mind of the analyst.

However much the analyst may persuade him or herself that these phenomena are inevitable, given the degree of the patient's pathology, he or she is nonetheless apparently far from understanding them. The analyst may experience enormous pressure to act, to change the setting, give up the analysis, suggest a termination date, or even persuade themselves that these phenomena are merely the result of the universal death drive and are to be permanently lived with. Such a clinical situation could be understood as the result of the impact on the analyst of the analysand's affects and projections.

But I think it is also indicative of a repetition of an essential 'core' breakdown of functioning, and the bringing of the more psychotic, or at any rate ill, aspects of the subject's personality for understanding. One could use the vague term 'breakdown' to cover what Winnicott described as the 'unthinkable state of affairs that underlies the defensive organization'.[1] It is, as he thought, a difficult term to define. It seems to involve both external signs that something is very wrong, and a view of the subject's inner experience of bewilderment and chaos. Winnicott also wrote of the fear of breakdown that has already been experienced, while here I am emphasizing the reality of the contemporary breakdown. He also wrote of the need for some subjects to experience primitive feelings associated with fear of breakdown, such as emptiness or loss of a sense of reality. Developing this notion, one could say that the clinical phenomena I have outlined cannot be eliminated, however well one analyses, however much transference and countertransference issues are examined, however sensitive the analyst. Indeed, there may even be a danger in being too understanding of the dynamics of the breakdown in communication at the point in the analysis when it first arises, for it may not then be experienced as a phenomenon to be understood. That is, there may be a need for the breakdown to be *felt* over a longish period by the analyst before it can be made tolerable to the analysand by a slow process of analysis.

The analysis of such ill people in adolescence poses particular clinical problems. While, in common with ill adults, they may be hard to reach, there is perhaps more hope of a favourable outcome. At least in adolescence there are the additional biological and social forces which are making the subject detach from the parents. Incestuous fantasies are also more readily available, and the adolescent is engaged in an active struggle around developing sexuality and the changing of his or her immature body into a mature sexual body; all of which makes the analytic relationship both crucial to the adolescent's future life and potentially very engaging. With the psychotic adolescent, one sees encapsulated a desperate struggle to achieve separation and independence, but one also sees the overwhelming guilt and sense of persecution when this normal developmental task cannot be successfully negotiated. I would see the breakdown of functioning at adolescence as essentially a developmental breakdown, as described by Laufer & Laufer:

> We define developmental breakdown in adolescence as the unconscious rejection of the sexual body and an accompanying feeling of being passive in the face of demands coming from one's own body, with the result that one's genitals are ignored or disowned or, in the more severe cases, the feeling that they are different from what one wanted them to be. It is a breakdown in the process of integrating the physically mature body image into the representation of oneself. Whatever the actual disorder, the specific interference in the developmental process that can be defined as adolescent pathology is contained in the adolescent's distorted view of and relationship to his body.[2]

I would add to this description the need to consider the infantile and childhood precursors of the adolescent breakdown which lay the ground for future disorder, as I shall indicate in the following clinical material.

Clinical Material

I shall try to highlight the core breakdown in communication in the following clinical material taken from the psychoanalysis of a self-mutilating adolescent. The analysis was undertaken at the Centre for Research into Adolescent Breakdown. My concept of a core breakdown arises both from my own case and from observation of some of the other cases in our research scheme. I noticed that at a certain point in the analysis several cases appeared to become apparently repetitive, with the same kind of material often being produced, while the analyst felt increasingly frustrated and sometimes tempted to do something active about the situation.

'Simon' came into analysis at the age of 17 following a suicide attempt. While feeling hopeless and depressed he had gone to a park and cut his wrists with a razor blade, with the intention of severing his arteries. He reported later that the pain of the cut stopped him. He had made an earlier attempt to cut an artery a year previously. The first overt sign of disturbance had been at puberty at the age of 13, when he had also probably attempted suicide, by suffocation in a plastic bag. Before his analysis, he cut himself superficially on his chest, abdomen, arms, and legs. As well as feeling generally depressed, he felt sexually and physically inadequate, particularly following a rejection by a girl he liked; and he was greatly troubled by sexual feelings and fantasies. Related to his sexual anxieties, Simon described intense self-hatred, particularly a hatred of and wish to disown his body, which he felt was too feminine and not masculine enough. He wished at times he could have another body, highlighting the kind of disturbance described above by Laufer & Laufer.

However, his desires were never as extreme as to make him wish to want a sex change, as some adolescents may. Simon felt, during the time he was suicidal, that the barrier between himself and the world was too thin, as if it would not hold, and that this was linked to his wish to cut his skin. He also felt at times that everything was a fairyland, that is unreal, and that he felt himself inadequate and separated from others, from those with normal sexuality and a normal life, by a glass barrier. He experienced periods of being over-whelmed with aggressive fantasies towards girls, for example, of wanting to rape them violently. Perhaps related to these fantasies, he had some homosexual experiences before analysis, which included oral and mutual masturbation, though apparently not anal penetration, which in the experience of the Brent Centre is of more prognostic significance regarding the adolescent's future sexual orientation. Simon's adolescent rebellious side was in evidence in the first year or so of the analysis in the way that he dressed garishly and aggressively, with various violent punk slogans daubed all over his clothes, as well as with a preoccupation with far-left politics and drugs.

Simon is from a middle-class background. His father had severe alcohol problems when Simon was a child, and he remained a degraded figure in the family. Neither parent supported the analysis; they felt that he would simply grow out of his problems and unfortunately chose to ignore the seriousness of his suicide attempts and self-mutilation. There is an interesting story about his mother's pregnancy with him, which came up earlier in the analysis as an aside, but whose significance became clearer only later in the analysis, when communication seemed 'dead'. It was said that his mother had a miscarriage while pregnant with him, yet the pregnancy continued despite the expulsion of an umbilical cord, and a twin was aborted.

To my surprise, the analysis began smoothly, and Simon developed a fairly strong therapeutic alliance. He usually arrived on time and began to feel that the analysis was the most crucial experience of his life. But after a few months, he began to feel constantly tempted to drop out. He felt that interpretations were aimed at brainwashing him and robbed him of his individuality. He spent many sessions trying to engage me, if not batter me, with a far-left extreme political discourse rather than a personal discourse. My attitude to the intensity with which he held his beliefs, as he felt, in opposition to psychoanalysis, was very much coloured by the fact that he was an adolescent and needed to experiment with ideologies. I also tended to respect the defensive aspect of his politics and tried to see what one could find in it that was personal to him. More worryingly regarding his mental stability, he tended to produce what I called 'propaganda for mindlessness' in which psychedelic drug experiences, particularly at weekends, were used repeatedly to eliminate any feelings of separation and dependency. There was at that time little sense that he had an awareness of the loss of an object – when I was not in his presence, I was almost completely absent from his mind. It seemed at such times that he was taken over by an idealized identification with a destructive and drunken father, as well as taken over by a mother whom he felt was driving him mad and whom he could not limit.

There was considerable material in the sessions, but quite often I had the feeling that, though he was talking about himself, he was trying to slip out of my reach; yet he also wished me to pursue him. He seemed to be attempting to seduce me into colluding with him – for example, by wishing me to endorse his drug abuse or ignore his suicidal impulses. I had to keep reminding myself of the seriousness of his difficulties, particularly around holiday times, as he was a suicide risk for at least the first 18 months of treatment. I had the impression that as soon as I became a relatively non-persecuting father in the transference, Simon would quickly react by cutting off what he was saying or would turn to drugs or alcohol outside the sessions, which I think could be understood as having to ward off an awareness of the pre-oedipal mother. I would suggest that such quick reactions to the transference changes mean having to pay constant attention in a vigilant way to what happens between sessions and from session to session, which one would not normally do with less ill patients.

Core Breakdown

As the analysis continued, Simon's more florid difficulties appeared to lessen; he did not cut himself, became less acutely suicidal, stopped turning to drugs, and sought some employment. In the first year or so of the analysis, he had short relationships with girls, but they, like him, attacked their bodies in various ways, e.g., through drug abuse, repeated abortions, or anorexia nervosa.

Subsequently, he formed a relationship that has lasted some years with a somewhat deprived but apparently caring young woman. The atmosphere of the sessions became less of a fight about brainwashing and instead rather more concerned with his inner world.

However, while he was making some moves in the outside world, the analysis began to become increasingly bogged down, an experience common to the analyses of several disturbed adolescents in analysis under the Centre for Research into Adolescent Breakdown. Simon would often not talk, justifying his silences by expressing a wish to overturn any progress, as well as wanting to make me powerless and so paralyze me. He would produce dreams, many of which seemed significant, but he would tend to analyze them himself. The dreams in themselves became a barrier to communication as much as a source of unconscious material. The sessions became increasingly boring and confusing, which could be seen, given his history, as a repetition in the transference of a broken-down father and a confused mother. The move towards heterosexuality with his girlfriend triggered in him a stonewalling attitude, of which he was hardly conscious. He was, however, aware of a dominant wish to lose his individuality, to be almost submerged in me, or dependent on me, 'like a leech,' as he put it.

Despite my interpretations, he might endlessly ruminate in a tedious way about things he should or should not do, which seemed to take all the meaning out of things, so much so that I was constantly losing the thread of the communications. This contrasted with the earlier part of the analysis, when I felt that, despite the enormous difficulties, such as having to face the possible risk of suicide or a severe psychotic breakdown, I was, by and large, in touch with what was going on. Simon said that he was like a child who was intent on not budging or moving an inch. He yearned for me to be God-like, to solve his problems, take away his pain, get him a job, and so on.

During a summer break, I took some time to think about what had been happening. I was aware that the other analysts in the research programme had been having somewhat similar experiences. In retrospect, I felt that I had been exposed to a relentless attempt to deaden me, and that it might be important to clarify this process. In addition, I had a fruitful consultation with a senior analyst, something which seems to be necessary on occasions in the treatment of such ill people, and which in this case helped the treatment to move along.

My deadness seemed to be an important phenomenon, as it dominated the sessions from my point of view and contrasted with the animation I experienced earlier in the analysis. It was as if Simon felt that he could not live without deadening or even destroying the other, and that this might help to account for his terror of living and of growing through adolescence into adulthood. What happened to the analysis at this time is difficult to summarize as it took several months of slow work to alter the picture. However, there was some immediate relief when I took up his fear that his leaving home and seeking some independence would result in his parents collapsing into a severe depression, and that communication between people contained the threat of death. The boredom of many of the sessions corresponded to how Simon kept his potency and intelligence away from the sessions, displaying them only in dreams. I began to realize that I had often experienced a fight to stay alive in the sessions, while all my 'nourishment' was being taken away by some sadistic process. The next theme that seemed to make an impact on him was that he was living at a price, that he could only just about bear being alive to his body and to others, that too much life was unbearable. The atmosphere of the sessions began to change. In part this might have been due to my own renewed confidence in the analytic process that had perhaps been compromised by the relentless deadening; but it was I believe also because we began to approach the heart of his pathology. I do not think that my renewed confidence could have sustained any significant or long-lasting change in him. One could say that, once he was fully established in the analysis, and in a long-term relationship with a girl, as well as in employment, his core disturbance, around which his symptoms had crystallized, was repeated in the transference.

It was then that the piece of history about his having survived a dead twin seemed to make sense. It appeared that I had become, in the transference, the dead twin, or the mother preoccupied by the dead twin. Rather to my surprise, Simon reacted with relief to this reconstruction, both immediately in one session and after it. I had imagined that he might not know what I was talking about; but on the contrary it seemed to make sense to him in a way that made one feel it had the ring of truth about it. It might have helped to see the themes I have described at an earlier stage; but then the point I am making is that I had to experience the deadness for it to be a clinical phenomenon pressing to be understood. In addition, it is possible that Simon would not have been able to make sense of the reconstruction without having gone through with me the experience of the period of core breakdown. I had taken up on previous occasions his murderousness and violence – one could hardly ignore it in view of the attacks on his body through cutting and drug taking, his attraction to violent politics and the punk way he used to dress early on in the analysis – but I had not understood the importance of the dead twin material nor had it been picked up by discussions at the Brent Centre.

I must emphasize that I am not assigning all his pathology to his early history, but that its emergence in the transference marked an important moment in the analysis. I should also clarify that I am not saying that the patient remembered the dead twin, though its significance rang many bells for him, or that an infant can remember such an event. It is possible that the latter is the case, but I leave the question open. It is more likely that the fact of the aborted twin became an integral part of the family's fantasy life, shaping and distorting their relationships. The change that took place in the analysis was, then, due to a complex mixture of a number of elements – my own under-standing had been increased, it was possible to face his deadening within the transference in a way that made sense to him and without him having to deny it or deaden the insight, and it was possible to make what seemed a relevant and emotionally significant reconstruction of his history. All these elements added together brought a sense of relief to both of us and enabled the analysis to progress, although I must emphasize that the analysis remained difficult and at times stressful for both of us.

I will present material from two sessions, separated by a few months, both of which contain a dream, in order to give a feel of what happened after the breakdown of communication. In a session after a job interview, Simon began with a vivid *dream* which horrified him.

He was standing outside his parents' house, talking to a three-foot-tall dwarf with incredibly well-developed muscles. As he talked to him, the dwarf shrank, becoming smaller and smaller, until he was six to seven inches high, like some sort of plastic doll, but still with incredible muscles, which the dwarf wanted Simon to inspect. The dwarf kept on talking, and all his flesh disappeared and ended up as just a few bones, which were not human but the remains of someone's dinner, the bones from a lamb chop.

He thought that the dwarf was a parody of himself – weight-lifting muscles on a small body. I took up how he felt dwarfed by me and belittled. This led on to him saying that I was the dwarf of the dream. He admired my superior-ity, but I was made smaller and smaller into a plastic doll, and then I was just like the remains of the dinner, nothing much left at all. I took up his (oral) devouring quality, how he stripped the food he had from me, leaving him feeling empty and only left with the scraps. This uncovered his horrifying wish to devour me, as he put it, in order to get close to me; as well as his fear that I would want to keep him with me and not let him go and get jobs and separate from me; as if I wanted him for me, so that he remain a dwarfed man with a small penis, 'an adult trapped in a child-size body,' as he put it.

In this frightening world, his fantasy was that I could only survive because of my 'good muscles'; but he then ate me up, which made him feel disgust and horror. If he took nourishment from me, it was only at the cost of survival. The more he took from the analytic feed, the smaller I became. The plastic doll may have been a reference to the dead girl twin, with whom he was identified in his presenting symptom of self-mutilation. There was also the fear of having a live communication with me. The moment he felt alive in the session, or that I was alive, he tended to cut off the discourse.

Between this session and the next one I shall summarize, Simon changed his job from one in which he was isolated from people to one which involved considerable contact with them. This seemed to parallel an impression I had that he felt rather better, less cut off, less guilt-ridden and anxious about com-municating. He also survived a break from the analysis rather better than usual, in that he did not have to increase his alcohol consumption danger-ously or smoke heavily, as he would usually do.

He began this session with another *dream*.

He was at his previous [isolated] job. The supervisor he didn't like was in the wrong office. A girl made a mistake which Simon tried to cover up in order to protect her. He was then at a market stall with a male friend. Some Indian bread turned out to be cake. His friend and he were both smartly dressed and walking across a ploughed field. They were worried about getting their clothes covered in mud.

His associations were that all the images in the dream were somehow inappropriate – the wrong office, the mistake, the wrong food, the wrong clothes. He wondered if he were saying something about her. After a pause, he thought there was something about being blamed for something he didn't do, by someone he hated, like the supervisor who was a bully. There was a feeling of guilt. The clothes made him feel out of place … there was shit on them. Then he recalled that he used to have a strong fear of eating in front of people that had got better recently … I then made an interpretation based on both the dream and his associations. I took up the feeling of a lack of fit with me and how he seemed to be feeling guilty and responsible for the lack of fit, as in the mistakes in the dream. He replied by saying that this was a feeling he always carried with him, not fitting in, being different … he was to blame for it all. The thing about his clothes not being right also referred to the feeling about his body not being right, which he used to get a lot. He wondered why he should have difficulty about eating in public. Was it the same?

I was thinking at this time about some recent sessions in which he had brought up quite primitive fears of eating up his mother's goodness, and so I felt fairly confident about bringing up that he might be expressing a fear of showing his aggressiveness in public, and that eating food was somehow linked to eating up his mother's food; and I also at some point linked this with a fear that he was responsible for the death of his twin. He did not, as he might have, greet this latter interpretation with scepticism; instead, it reminded him that his mother had often expressed to him, as a child, that she would have liked another child after him. This led to his fear that he had destroyed her babies, and strangely he recalled that for years he had hated milk and dairy products. For example, he never took milk in tea or coffee and always hated cheese, the smell of which made him feel sick. He admitted with much hesitation that the eating up of his twin was a lurking fantasy. He blamed himself for his mother not having more children. He was her 'cute little boy,' which made him grow up feeling like a selfish little monster.

He returned spontaneously to the dream and the sense of inappropriateness. The friend with him always had smart clothes, and Simon had wondered whether he was gay, because he came across as effeminate and ambiguous sexually. It made him think that while he himself was a child, it was almost like being a girl. I brought him back to the male supervisor in the dream and made some reference to his father. Simon said that this man was gay. He was then not a good father who could help, or 'not a real man,' as he put it. And the session ended.

The following session, Simon described what he had felt about this session, which I thought was quite useful. He said he had felt freer than usual that usually he feels in a kind of straitjacket, when he has to talk about one thing at a time and cannot see the links between things: that he often feels as if he is undergoing an exam, or he is not free, or can't express himself as 'me.' But this time he felt he could talk about himself without those feelings, he was less cut off, and less anxious. I certainly thought that he was beginning to work through the issue of separation and independence, the right he had to live and the dreadful feeling of being responsible for killing off both his twin and his mother's other babies. The new job which gave him access to people seemed a concrete manifestation of some inner change.

Discussion

As I suggested in the introduction, it might be useful to distinguish various kinds of breakdown in communication to highlight the kind of problem that I have made the theme of the paper. I should say that one or more of the following kinds of breakdown in communication are bound to arise at various points of an analysis. I also make no claim for exhaustiveness and am merely offering this typology for convenience.

Analysand's Resistance

Some breakdowns in communication are usually of short duration, as is the case when the analysand's free associations fail due to a resistance, including a transference resistance. Freud wrote at these moments that the associations really cease and are not merely being kept back owing to ordinary feelings of unpleasure,

> ... if a patient's free associations fail the stoppage can invariably be removed by an assurance that he is being dominated at the moment by an association which is concerned with the doctor himself or with something connected with him. As soon as the explanation is given, the stoppage is removed, or the situation changed from one in which the associations fail into one in which they are being kept back.[3]

I think that the implication of this quotation is that these kinds of breakdowns in communication are transient and fairly easily dealt with. Whether or not we would now consider that giving an assurance of the type indicated invariably leads to a freeing of communication is perhaps debatable. What seems to be the point is that one's first line of approach is often to think of the breakdown as a resistance. If the breakdown persists for longer, then one may have to reconsider what is going on in the session.

Negative Therapeutic Reaction

This notion seems to designate a particular clinical phenomenon where an improvement or temporary suspension of symptoms produces in the analysand an exacerbation of their pathology, resistance, or hostility: '...the need for illness has got the upper hand ... over the desire for recovery.'[4]

Freud considered that the phenomenon was the expression of an unconscious sense of guilt. In Kleinian theory, the phenomenon seems to be the result of an exacerbation of envy of therapeutic progress. Betty Joseph[5] has described what she calls 'addiction to near death' in a small group of patients. They often show a strong negative therapeutic reaction but this is only part of a broader and more insidious picture. There is a powerful addiction to masochism, and a particular way of communicating this to the analyst. Some kinds of sado-masochistic transferences may incur repeated negative therapeutic reactions. The sadistic part of the patient cannot tolerate any good being sustained.

Phenomena associated with the negative therapeutic reaction seem to be long-lasting and do imply that there has to be some kind of improvement in the first place. In the ill adolescent, it is difficult to be certain of any major positive change. One could perhaps describe briefer moments of 'undoing' the analytic work, from day to day, or week to week; this is not quite a negative therapeutic reaction but is perhaps related to it.

The Analyst's Resistance

This category basically describes breakdowns of communication that are to be avoided. Herbert Rosenfeld described in meticulous detail the kinds of difficulties that the analyst can get into when treating psychotic subjects, and which result in a negative 'impasse' or treatment failure. He is essentially referring to a kind of impasse in which 'severe negative reactions to analysis do not follow real progress and where it would not, therefore, be appropriate to speak of negative feelings being due to envy of therapeutic progress.'[6] He felt that the source of such difficulties often arose in the analyst. They could be due to constantly vague or badly timed interpretations, rigidity or inflexibility, and above all to unrecognized difficulties in the analyst's countertransference. He thought it important to distinguish between a subject communicating clearly with symbolic language and the confused way of talking of a psychotic subject who has lost their way in the analysis. 'Most psychotic subjects,' he writes, 'project their feelings and anxieties very intensely into the analyst when they verbally or non-verbally communicate. This generally helps the analyst to understand better. But if the analyst cannot cope with the patient's projections, he tends to get out of touch.'[7]

John Klauber[8] implied that some kinds of breakdown in communication follow from a lack of sympathy between patient and analyst. This could be a result of inevitable differences in personality, or the analyst failing to recognize his or her unconscious need for sympathy with and from the patient, or alternatively that he pitches all his interpretations at one level. Thus, Klauber, like Rosenfeld, is warning analysts not to be too rigid or inflexible in their approach.

Particular Kinds of Transference

There are particular kinds of transference that run the risk of creating breakdowns in communication between analyst and analysand. For example, with the kind of person who may need the analyst to be a 'parent who was not able to tune accurately into his feelings, who was continually concerned with his or her sense of failure or inability to cope, or who was continually criticizing or belittling him.'[9]

I also think that there is a particular kind of 'split transference,' in which to put it simply, the internal parents are not united and are constantly and strongly divided. This internal splitting makes the analysis of such subjects particularly tricky as they may unconsciously use the split transference to ward off interpretations. The moment one gets close to one aspect of the transference, another aspect is used to cut off any work and so must be simultaneously addressed.

Finally, there may be breakdowns in communication related to a transference of a psychotic parent who, one could say, never had the analysand in mind, and where there have been major breakdowns in early care.

Core Breakdown in Communication

I have already described the observations that led me to put forward the notion of a core breakdown of communication. I am basically describing a transference phenomenon, with possibly multiple origins from early childhood right through to puberty and later adolescence. It is possible that such a phenomenon arises in a definite form only when the personality structure is beginning to become fixed, from about mid-adolescence onwards. I have emphasized that the breakdown needs to be tolerated by the analyst, in the face of temptations to turn to what one could call 'false' solutions, such as trying unusual analytic technique or interventions. Part of the origin of the phenomenon may be attributed to primitive areas of the psyche on the lines described both by Winnicott in his fear of breakdown paper and by Balint in his book *The Basic Fault*.[10] Balint's concept of the basic fault refers to a pre-oedipal level of the mind, which involves an exclusively two-person relationship. While the patient functions at this level, the analyst may fail to be in touch with the patient who may then experience feelings of emptiness and deadness. My notion of a core breakdown does not necessarily refer only to such primitive levels of functioning. Indeed, there is no evidence that Simon or the other adolescents in the research were regressed at the point of core breakdown. On the contrary, Simon, for example, was progressing well in the outside world.

Presumably, however, this may have allowed him to bring more primitive material to my attention. I am, anyway, calling attention to an apparent interruption in the analytic process, which needs to be worked through. I am also suggesting that the way in which the analyst may be forced to be out of touch with the patient is in itself significant. In addition, I am not suggesting that the analyst encourage regression in order to heal the primitive areas of the psyche, though there may be times when this is important. Instead, I am suggesting that, like it or not, the analyst may find himself out of touch when he treats such ill patients and may mistakenly wish to do something unusual about this. Presumably at such times the patient communicates a quality of despair and hopelessness that appears to demand action by someone. The analyst may then feel that his presence is not enough. But it is possible that he may then, if unusual interventions are attempted, miss an opportunity really to grasp the significance of this moment in the analysis and this may then merely repeat some basic fault in the patient's early history.

Returning in summary to Simon's analysis, it seems to underline a difficult and common dilemma – about how to communicate with someone who has great problems in communication. How, one may ask, can one communicate with the primitive, psychotic-like areas – represented in his case by the dead twin? That is, putting it metaphorically, how can one get in touch with a dead twin who has been aborted and cannot speak? Simon's discourse seemed to turn round and round this essential dilemma, and the cost of attempting to communicate – the cost of sanity. The analyst has to bear the psychotic cutting off of emotions, in Simon's case the dead transference. This transference was composed of several dead figures, not only the dead twin but also the mother deadened to Simon's needs, her dead babies and the father anaesthetized by alcohol to Simon's emotions.

In my summary of different kinds of breakdown in communication, I made the point that some kinds of breakdown are inevitable while others, mainly due to the analyst's resistance, are to be avoided. The point I wish to make is that with the ill adolescent, and perhaps the ill adult, the core pathology needs to be experienced in the transference for treatment to be effective, and that the way that this may occur is via a breakdown of communication of the type I have outlined. Rather than the periods of deadness and difficulty being seen as an absence of analytic work, they may in fact be indicative of the subject's attempt to work through something, or at the very least to bring, unconsciously, to the analyst's attention some important areas that need to be addressed. Other less ill subjects may be able to do this in a less disordered fashion. There may be many resistances, even the occasional severe breakdown in communication, but not the all-pervasive disturbance in communication. The treatment of the ill adolescent of the kind I have described is very demanding and difficult, for the analyst's own capacity to stay alive and sane is constantly being challenged.

Notes

1 Winnicott (1974).
2 Laufer and Laufer (1984, pp. 22–23).
3 Freud (1912, p. 104).
4 Freud (1923, p. 49).
5 Joseph (1982).
6 Rosenfeld (1987, p. 139).
7 Rosenfeld (1987, p. 51).
8 Klauber (1976).
9 King (1978, p. 331).
10 Balint (1968).

7 Becoming a Psychoanalyst – Which Home to Go to?

There are many difficulties in the path of becoming a psychoanalyst. I shall aim to explore some of these difficulties, with the hope that we may find some overlapping consensus in our different ways of working encapsulated in those different words, training and formation – the former implying more emphasis on acquiring a professional skill, and the latter more about developing an identity. I think students need both these elements, in order to 'become a psychoanalyst,' but there are different views about how and where they acquire them.

I will unpeel the basic logic of the Eitingon model of training (from now on 'EM') and see how this model is working now. Of course, I can only speak in detail about the British Psychoanalytical Society, the source of my own formative experience as a psychoanalyst. I also have to say that there are several different 'logics' in the EM, not some easily unifying principle, because of the way that the model developed at a particular time in the development of the psychoanalytic movement, when there were threats to its existence, worries about splits and schisms, and a wish to extend its influence internationally. There was undoubtedly a need for psychoanalysis to become organized and for its education to become more formalized if it were to face the challenges of life in the early 20th century. One may ask if this is still the case. I suspect it is, even more so with all the competition from alternative therapies and psychologies, but it is still perhaps a question worth considering.

The context for considering the EM is, no doubt, the current crisis in the application of the EM, brought about by the controversial decision of the IPA Board to allow societies following the EM to reduce the number of sessions required for a training analysis from 4/5 to 3 times a week. Some French analysts had written to the IPA President, expressing concern for how the 'French model' was invoked tendentiously, without considering the complexities of the rest of the French context.

The proposal itself has unleashed considerable anger and anxiety and opened up once more international fault lines in how psychoanalysis is practiced. One member of the Board told me that it's going to be a 'blood bath,' but they were not sure whose blood was going to be spilled. Only time will tell.

DOI: 10.4324/9781003683315-7

I suspect that from the outside these disputes could appear to be unbelievably trivial in a world where there is currently such conflict, turmoil, and intolerance. I hardly think it is an exaggeration to maintain that currently fears about the economic and political stability of society, the threat of 'foreign' invasion, and a tendency for societies and majorities in whole nations to turn inwards, predominates many Western countries, at times creating an ugly atmosphere of suspicion and prejudice towards those perceived as different and hence dangerous. Such fears seem to mirror old arguments, going back centuries to the early Enlightenment thinkers and even before, when the parameters of discussion about tolerance were mainly around religious tolerance. Realistic threats about terrorism, spilling over into irrational 'populist' movements preoccupied by threats from 'abroad,' economic fears about being swamped by millions of immigrants taking jobs and burdening services and such like, all echo many of the preoccupations of the times when religious wars and fears of society being plunged into chaos by heresies or by radical thinkers abounded, putting societies, as now, into considerable conflict. The current debates about different psychoanalytic models have a flavour of these religious disputes. Yet one cannot ignore the wider context for this current crisis, especially as I have heard that there are, in part at least, 'economic' reasons driving the proposed changes – due to the assertion that people can no longer afford to pay for more than three sessions a week.

Perhaps what is often forgotten in such economic arguments is that, as John Klauber put it,

> the cause of psychoanalysis demands the recognition of the length of time that human development takes – for the patient and for the analyst – and the toleration of apparent therapeutic failures which may prove to be considerable successes in terms of the patient's inner life and even bring direct therapeutic rewards after many years.[1]

We are in for the *longue durée*.

But prior to looking at the EM model, I would suggest that one needs to look first at what sort of facilitating environment we think best for our students. What are we looking for in our students, and what sort of reflective space do we think is possible and compatible with our psychoanalytic thinking? What is the purpose of the training – is it for the benefit of the student or for their patients? Or both? Whose welfare is paramount, analyst or patient? That is, should we safeguard the student's welfare at all costs? What about the welfare of the patients who trust us to help them? How are these different responsibilities maintained? Where does 'external' monitoring come in, if at all? And finally, how far should students be actively involved in shaping their experience?

To begin to answer these difficult questions, I have elsewhere argued[2] that a fear of a loss of home, or more fundamentally a fear of a loss of a psychic structure which provides a central core of our identity – a *psychic home* – accounts for a certain amount of prejudiced and intolerant attitudes to those perceived as different. I would suggest that these debates about different psychoanalytic requirements for students raise fundamental issues about *belonging*, about the nature of one's own psychic home, the kinds of identifications that make up the psychic home, and fears about its loss, or its being changed beyond recognition – hence my subtitle, 'Which home to go to?' So, to what sort of 'analytic home' do we think our students should or could belong?

This sense of a home pervades much of our work at various levels. Like our patients, we psychoanalysts carry our psychic home with us, though it will manifest itself differently. We may not reveal details of our private life to our patients, but we carry our psychic home with us into the session. Our choice of interior design of the consulting room, not to mention the books and any objects, may well reflect the nature of our psychic home; there is an interaction between the subjectivity of the analyst and the interior space where they work. An alive psychic home can provide a sustaining space for the analyst, allowing them to cope with the inevitable loneliness of the work.

While the analytic work carries on in separate localities, that of the analyst and that of the patient, they do intertwine in various ways, in a dynamic fashion. Sometimes the analyst may find that their psychic home is invaded by the patient, with little space to think or feel; or else there may be a confusion of spaces, with little sense of a boundaried psychic home. These experiences may occur at once or take time to develop through the strange unfolding of the transference and countertransference.

A patient comes into our consulting room for the first meeting. We may have spoken to them briefly on the telephone, or communicated by email, perhaps have found out a little about them, either directly or from a referring colleague. But the fact is, both analyst and patient are strangers to one another in several ways, both regarding their lives and cultures, but also regarding their strange unconscious inner life. We provide a potential home for the expression of this inner life, for a hopefully alive engagement of the analyst and patient's psychic homes.

I think this is the place where issues of training or formation begin – with what is essential in the analytic encounter, and whether what is essential can be carried over into what it takes to become a psychoanalyst. So before going into some of the specifics of the EM, I think it may be helpful to make some general points about the dilemmas of analytic training, formation, or preparation for entering the particular home provided by a psychoanalytic organization.

Dilemmas of Training

I think that whatever the shape of an analytic training, it does need to help prepare the potential psychoanalyst with tools for tolerating considerable conflict, both at the clinical and the organizational level. At the clinical level, this means, for example, helping the patient's ego to tolerate the mainly unconscious conflicts that arise as part of the analytic work, while the analyst must bear the strain of keeping in mind conflicting levels both in themselves and in what they hear from the patient. This involves on the analyst's part considerable strain, the *strain of restraint*. It can be traumatic listening to and bearing with the patient's very painful experiences day in and day out, and this can be very challenging at the beginning of one's analytic career, before one finds a relatively secure analytic identity. It is difficult bearing the *loneliness* of the consulting room and the frustrations of having to be constantly restrained emotionally with patients. I tackle this issue in detail in the next chapter. We have to bear the cost of having to hold onto hate and love for the patient. We hope that our students can become capable of bearing such considerable strains, relatively free from undue influence and without resorting to formulaic interpretations, a common form of defence against uncertainty.

Then there is the constant interplay, or duality, between the need for the analyst to keep to certain rules and boundaries and the need to be receptive to the primary process laws of the unconscious, to listen to the unconscious. For the analyst to come down too much on one side of this duality would be a technical error. Excessive rigidity of technique, or on the contrary, excessive intrusion into the patient's unconscious may be damaging to patient and analyst. Or to put this dilemma another way, a fear of being seduced by the patient in a negative way may make us idealize technique as a defence. Such idealization of technique may make analysts convey to students in supervisions and seminars that there is only one way of doing analysis, *their* way.

There is also the problem about how to find a balance between the years of preparation needed to master an exacting conceptual system and technique while also being able to maintain personal freedom from the weight of authority.

Here one comes up against the inevitable organizational conflicts, which do impact on students; they cannot be avoided, whatever one does to try to minimize their influence. Leaving aside for the moment whether the organization uses a training analyst model, any psychoanalytical organization will have to come to terms with the problem of how to manage the power of the unconscious. Working with the unconscious can be a bit like working with toxic radiation; only we must allow ourselves to be contaminated by the toxic material, up to a point, of course. And there may be a point where the toxicity becomes too much to bear. Psychoanalytic organizations seem constantly to run the risk of becoming toxic to their members. Then the analytic home can become the scene of intense family squabbles.

The institutional behaviour of analysts and how they function within a particular society is a complex matter. Historical factors would need to be considered, not only a particular society's foundation history and social context, but also the early history of psychoanalysis, where one could say the acting out of unconscious forces permeated the personal relationships of those involved, making them at times very toxic. Freud feared that psychoanalysis would become adulterated or tainted by 'heresy,' by the personal views of particular heretics. In London, of course, we had the Controversial Discussions centred on whether Melanie Klein was a heretic or an innovative genius but essentially faithful to Freud. In France, they have had the pivotal role of Jacques Lacan who, in the context of a rigid Paris Society of the time, argued for a radical 'return to Freud' and, in particular, the close connection between language and the unconscious.

Time and again one can see in these controversies how the personal element of psychoanalysis may become detached, or split off, from the analytic function and then acted out destructively in institutional settings. Of course, there are always personal differences between analysts and these become magnified in what are often relatively small organizations. But alongside the detachment of the personal element in practicing psychoanalysis, there may be a fear of integration of the personal and the rule-based aspects of psychoanalysis.

Here one comes to what Michael Parsons[3] has described in detail in his pivotal paper, 'Forming an identity,' as the strain in training where the personal needs of the student for their own analysis come up against the needs of the organization to provide some sort of appropriate structure for the student to learn about psychoanalysis. The *personal* and the *institutional* elements of training or formation need to be considered but their integration is far from easy and will inevitably impose strains on all involved. The different models have different solutions as to where the personal and the institutional aspects of the student experience take place, but the strains cannot be avoided.

I certainly agree that the crucial issue for students, and indeed for all of us as we grow into becoming analysts, is that of finding our own genuine analytic identity or formation. All that the personal analysis can do, whether it is a training analysis under the EM or another model, is to start off a process that will need to continue well after the analysis has ended, as Klauber suggested.

The Eitingon Model

After this long preamble, but with some of these questions in mind, I will look at what I have been asked to consider, which is the 'logic' involved in the Eitingon model of analytic training.

To understand this rather complex logic, one needs to begin with some history about which I can only give a brief overview.

Max Eitingon set up the Berlin Polyclinic in 1920, with the aim of making psychoanalysis available to those who would not otherwise have been able to afford it. This responded to Freud's own wishes. In conjunction with this social role, the Polyclinic was at the outset seen as the platform for the training of psychoanalysts and psychoanalytic research. It provided patients for students and was also fundamental to the organization of the Berlin Psychoanalytic

Institute, as the London Clinic remains for the British Society to this day. As Freud described ten years after the foundation of the Berlin Institute:

> First, it endeavours to make our therapy accessible to the great multitude who suffer under their neuroses no less than the wealthy, but who are not in a position to meet the cost of their treatment. Secondly, it seeks to provide a centre at which analysis can be taught theoretically and at which the experience of older analysts can be handed on to pupils who are anxious to learn. And lastly, it aims at perfecting our knowledge of neurotic illnesses and our therapeutic technique by applying them and testing them under fresh conditions.[4]

Over a 20-year period Eitingon, initially with Abraham, established a *tripartite* training model consisting of a personal analysis, theoretical learning, and supervision, within the structure of an organizing Institute. This was a kind of psychoanalytic trade school, with the student as an apprentice. This setup became the point of reference for establishing training criteria for candidates under an International Training Commission under the auspices of the IPA. It was Eitingon who affirmed most comprehensively the absolute requirement of undergoing personal analysis prior to entering the profession. Freud had earlier written about the requirements for an analyst:

> It is not enough for this that he himself should be an approximately normal person [ein annähernd normaler Mensch]. It may be insisted, rather, that he should have undergone a psycho-analytic purification [Purifizierung] and have become aware of those complexes of his own which would be apt to interfere with his grasp of what the patient tells him.[5]

And Eitingon wrote that:

> We are all firmly convinced with only too good reason, that henceforth no one who has not been analyzed must aspire to the rank of a practicing analyst.[6]

One presumes that 'with only too good reason' refers to all the personal troubles that the psychoanalytic pioneers had encountered when having to deal with the 'toxic' effects of the unconscious at work both with their patients but also with one another, which called for Freud's rather desperate 'psychoanalytic purification.' Of course, what Freud means by 'an approximately normal person' is a matter of debate, especially given the evidence of the unruly group behaviour of psychoanalysts, both then and now.

There were, then, probably several motives for creating this training model. There was a genuine social concern underlying the foundation of the Berlin

Polyclinic, and that concern can easily be forgotten. There was a realization that psychoanalysis needed to recruit more people if it were to survive, and hence the need to promote a training that could attract doctors and give them a credible professional qualification, and the training did succeed in this aim and became the accepted international training model for many years. There was recognition of the need to do scientific research if psychoanalysis were to survive and research requires some kind of organized facilities. And there were also fears and fantasies, some realistic and some more likely psychotic, that without a strong training structure, psychoanalysis would become flooded with 'wild,' uncontained, and downright 'mad' analysts, irreparably damaging psychoanalysis's already precarious reputation.

But in addition, imbedded within the Berlin training model, there were several problematic tensions, which interacted in various ways, and which are still active today. First, there was a certain amount of idealization, with Eitingon claiming that such trainings must work 'carefully and untiringly to preserve and further develop what our Founder has created.'[7] Second, the issue of training soon became embroiled with the issue of lay analysis, in part because of the situation in the United States, where only doctors were allowed to train. There was a real fear the psychoanalytic community would split apart on this issue. Thirdly, authorization to train was taken away from individual analysts and transferred to a collective body within each society, the Training Committee, which then often became the real centre of power within the societies. And finally, another source of potential conflict around matters of power and control concerned who had the authority within the psychoanalytic community to authorize the training procedures and requirements – the individual society or the IPA. In the event, as we know the Americans resisted lay analysis for many years, while societies in Europe were more open to non-medical colleagues. Certainly, in the British Society, a substantial number of lay analysts, many of them, women, have played crucial parts in developing psychoanalytic theory and practice – such as Anna Freud, Melanie Klein, Ella Sharpe, Susan Isaacs, Pearl King, Marion Milner, etc.

Essential to the EM model and the focus of debates, then and now, about how to 'become a psychoanalyst' is, of course, the role of the personal analysis, the training analysis, or 'control' or 'instructional,' or 'didactic' analysis, depending upon different translations of the original *Lehr-* or *didaktische Analyse*. By conquering his own neurosis, the analyst to be would protect patients from his own countertransference and resistance. It is worth mentioning here that from the beginning there were contrasting views about the place of the training analysis. While all agreed that a personal analysis was a requirement for becoming an analyst, there were those like Ferenczi who insisted that there was no difference between a therapeutic and training analysis, except that the latter had to be as deep as possible for the good of potential patients, which seemed to imply that analysts were to become some 'super beings.' Others, like Eitingon, considered that the training analysis was distinguished from the therapeutic analysis not by a difference in technique but by an extra intention that it assumes or receives by virtue of the fact that the student is effectively required to learn something from their training analyst.

There were also differences in view about when the training analysis should end and whether or not there should be overlap between the analysis and the course of theoretical learning and supervision, with, for example, the Vienna Society preferring their candidates to have finished their analysis before the course and others insisting they needed to be in analysis during the course and while seeing patients, so as to bring issues into their analysis to help deal with personal issues arising from seeing patients.

There seemed to be agreement that whenever the training analysis took place, it was to be conducted by only those especially chosen for their competence to do so, not just any analyst. In Berlin, the suitably named Hans Sachs, a lay analyst, became one of the first such 'master' analysts, analysing 25 candidates over a two-year period – of course the analysis only lasted for about a year. (I am of course making a reference to Wagner's master cobbler in Die Meistersinger von Nürnberg, who trained up the ad hoc apprentice Walther to win at the song contest and thereby win the hand of Eva Pogner.)

Already, the British were complaining that this was insufficient and that it should take at least two years! Sachs himself wrote of the training analysis as akin to religious initiation and the trial period for novitiates in the church. 'The didactic analysis opened him to the mysteries of the unconscious, after which the seeker would gaze upon the inner forces of the Oedipus complex, infantile sexuality, and human ambivalence.'[8]

As an antidote to the dangers of the training analysis, the formal educational system in Berlin, where students would have contact with other analysts and different perspectives, limited the training analyst's authority, in the hope of decreasing the student's reliance on their analyst. However, in Vienna, a student would be completely dependent on their analyst, who served as teacher, referrer, and research mentor.

Freud, as often, was rather ambivalent about the institutionalization of the personal analysis and the view of himself as infallible. However, he was also concerned about the future of psychoanalysis after the various painful secessions, and urged that, '...the new generation of analysts should learn to renounce part of their self-assertion and independence, to be educated to discipline and self-discipline and to accept an authority with the right and duty of instructing and warning.'[9] However, Freud, aware very much of the son's need to rebel against the father, had been less attentive about the wish of the Kronos-like desire of the father to destroy his sons.[10] Nonetheless, by the time of his paper *Analysis Terminable and Interminable* in 1937, Freud had become increasingly aware of the role that destructive forces play in life. Thinking of the power of the death drive, Freud addressed what one may hope for in psychoanalytic treatment of analysts themselves.

Analysts, he writes, are 'people who have learned to practice a particular art; alongside this they may be allowed to be human beings like anyone else.'[11] And that it was reasonable to expect an analyst to have a considerable degree of mental normality and correctness, which I assume implies decent ethical behaviour. They also should …

> possess some kind of superiority, so that in certain analytic situations he can act as a model for his patient and in others as a teacher. And finally we must not forget that the analytic relationship is based on a love of truth – that is, on a recognition of reality – and that it precludes any kid of sham or deceit.[12]

To achieve what he also describes as joining a probably 'impossible' profession because of these exacting demands, the analyst must have a personal analysis, which will inevitably be incomplete; indeed, he recommends reanalysis every five years to make sure the analyst does not become overwhelmed with the traumatic effect of listening to so much repressed material. The personal analysis will have accomplished its purpose if it gives the student a firm conviction of the existence of the unconscious, if it enables him, when repressed material emerges, to perceive in himself things which would otherwise be incredible to him and to give the student a sample of analytic technique. His own analytic work does not end with the personal analysis but needs to continue after the end of the analysis. The processes of 'remodelling the ego' should continue '*spontaneously* [my italics] in the analyzed subject,' making use of all subsequent experiences in a newly acquired way. So far as this happens, 'it makes the analyzed subject qualified to be an analyst himself.'[13]

And here we have encapsulated the difficult issue of the analyst's qualification to be an analyst – a capacity to continue self-analysis and to change after the actual analysis has ended. The qualified analyst has thus not so much arrived somewhere but has the means to continue the journey – a journey towards a sense of their own identity as analysts, a sense of authenticity perhaps. In that sense, analysis is about setting the student free in some way. Is this what a psychoanalytic society can do for its students? And if so, how is this to be accomplished? Any analytic society needs at least to address these difficult questions.

The British Experience

In this final section, I will share some of my personal impressions of the British Training (BT), both as a student and as a training analyst. I certainly think the issue of freedom and obstacles to freedom has been part and parcel of this experience. Its overall approach could be described as a team approach. The student is seen and usually assessed by a whole range of analysts in theoretical and clinical seminars, as well as the two training analyst supervisors of two five times a week cases from the clinic. The training analyst has no say in admission to the training, or progress or qualification. They used to have a say in the past and were obliged to make some sort of report on progress, as well as agree to the student taking on the two training patients at each stage, but no longer, though the training analyst still must agree to the student starting the seminar programme. The progress of the students is monitored individually by their Progress Advisor, and overall, by the Student Progress Committee, which has the responsibility for making a recommendation for qualification to the Education Committee, based predominantly on the supervisors' reports and, to a lesser extent, the reports from seminar leaders. Students are given feedback on a regular basis about their progress with the hope that any problems are picked up early and then dealt with accordingly, so that potential difficulties are addressed. There is no requirement at this level to present a written paper, though there is later for those who wish to become Fellows following membership. There is instead an emphasis on clinical practice in the consulting room and the ability to convey this by word of mouth.

Our training requires seminar leaders to report on the participants with a form estimating their capacity on different levels – participation in the seminar, clinical expertise, intellectual understanding, and emotional understanding. The students are also required to appraise the seminar leader's performance, with a group report to the curriculum committee, which is then sent to the leader.

To select candidates, there is: (1) an informal interview to see if they can go to the more formal stage of interviews, looking at qualifications, background, and motivation. If the candidate then applies to train, they fill in a form with their background and reasons for applying, plus a personal and professional reference. Then, (2) there are two formal interviews organized by the Admission Committee – two interviews with two different training analysts – looking at history, insight, analysability, and clinical experience. There is then a decision made to: A. accept for training; B. reject for training; C. reconsider (re-interview) after a period, for example, after a period of more analysis, if already in analysis, or after starting analysis. Rejected candidates have the right to have a feedback interview.

The choice of training analysts is very variable. Ultimately, it's a 'choice' for the candidate – some see more than one analyst before deciding, others are already in analysis with a training analyst and do not need to change analyst, others (like me!) prefer to be 'given' a training analyst with a particular orientation, I was 26 and just asked for an independent. The Student Progress Committee consists of several training analysts of different orientations; each member has two to three candidates as their responsibility. Members of the committee usually stay for three to four years before being replaced. The Chair is appointed by selection committee if there is competition, and is a member of the Education Committee, which has overall responsibility for the training.

Qualification is in the hands of the Student Progress Committee, after the supervisors have agreed that the student is ready, and all reports are sent to the committee, and a decision is then made. A student then automatically becomes an IPA analyst. But membership of the Society takes place by secret public ballot at the next Business Meeting of the Society – prior to an evening

Scientific Meeting, and with pre-circulated details provided. This is a formality, though in theory there could be a refusal to accept the analyst into the Society. It is, however, usually a pleasant occasion and followed by a drink celebration.

The BT retains the essential Eitingon tripartite elements of personal analysis, theoretical learning, and supervision, with a clinic making psychoanalysis available at low fees for the public, provided they accept analysis from a student under supervision. In fact, the clinic also offers low-fee consultations and some psychotherapy with qualified analysts as well as some subsidized analysis with those on the postgraduate 'Fellowship' course. On qualification, students become members and can later go on to become Fellows through undertaking a fellowship course, which ends with a clinical presentation. There are incidentally loans offered at low interest for students to help them with the costs of training.

A *training analysis* conducted by a training analyst remains central to the education of students and hence to understanding the logic of the BT. The role, practice, and selection of the training analyst have changed considerably over the years, but it still does remain a key element. In the 1950s, training analysts were asked by senior colleagues to join them, without formal selection. This would be based on what was known of their clinical skills through presentations, discussion, and papers, and some judgement of their character, their maturity, and, I suppose, their identification with one of the three groups – Freudian, Independent, and Kleinian. So, there was a clear political element of this selection. That is still true today to some extent, but only as far as anything in the organization of psychoanalysts is political.

For a time there were separate streams of training as part of the 'Gentleman's [or Gentlewoman's] agreement' to accommodate the tensions between groups, but that proved too difficult to maintain and there soon arose a unified training, but one where at that time there was an agreement to provide a balanced curriculum, one which reflected the different streams of British psychoanalysis. Incidentally, this balance has become more and more difficult to maintain.

Training analysts are now appointed through a rigorous selection process. They have to be Fellows with a certain experience, with a minimum of about 4,000 hours seeing 4–5× a week analytic cases, and hopefully with evidence of an engagement both with the Society's committees and in writing papers, books, or giving lectures. They will need a personal reference about their character and a professional reference about their practice. When I was appointed 30 years ago, I went to Eric Rayner one afternoon and went through all my clinical experience, talking about the different patients I had seen, so he could fully understand my approach. He already knew my work and thinking to some extent, as I had been part of a group of Independent analysts at different stages who had met once a term for a whole Sunday (the 'Sunday Group') to share ideas and think about our development. He and Pearl King were the two training analysts who were present at the meetings.

I should add that I now do something similar for younger analysts with another senior colleague, Jonathan Sklar, though our aim is a bit more focused in terms of helping younger analysts develop their sense of themselves within the Independent (Winnicottian) tradition and hopefully put themselves forward to the 'Training panel.'

An assessment of 'character' is, of course, a difficult matter, and there have been times when this has been very controversial. I was even involved in an appeal process when one candidate for becoming a training analyst was refused a training panel on the grounds of their character. This decision was contested. Interestingly, the appeal succeeded, but the analyst never reapplied.

The Training Staff Committee is responsible for appointing training analysts, and once they have met with a potential candidate informally and seen the application and references, they will agree to a training panel to evaluate the candidate.

A panel is formed of four training analysts, two from the analyst's own group and one each from the two other groups. Some candidates prefer not to have any named group member on the panel. Also, a candidate can veto a panel member if there are personal issues they feel will interfere with the panel's objectivity.

The panel involves the candidate presenting clinical material, usually a history and two sessions from a patient. After that, there will be some discussion about potential training issues. For example, what would they do if they felt they had a student in analysis about whom they were very concerned? How would they think about the issues that may arise?

There is no vote until the next Training Staff Committee responsible for this whole process meets. The chair of the panel (usually from the candidate's own group) will give a summary of what happened, and then the other panel members will add their account. There will be a discussion from the rest of the committee members, and then the panel itself has a secret vote. If there is a stalemate, the Chair of the committee can have a casting vote, but usually there are different ways of managing this situation, such as considering a further panel.

I have been on, or chaired, quite a few panels. They are usually actually very interesting occasions, where one can have a good clinical discussion with one's peers, and there are rarely tensions between groups, here at least. If the candidate is doing well, they usually join in with the discussion. If the panel members feel they must supervise the candidate, this usually means it's not going well.

What is the panel looking for? The Training Staff Committee has spent many hours trying to define this, and there are some criteria published on the members' website, as part of a policy of transparency, but in practice, it's not that easy to define. It's not just being a decent analyst but having a sense that this analyst can be entrusted to look after our candidates, who, in turn, must treat their training patients. Therefore, there is a sense that the Training analysis is not just a personal analysis, though that remains central, but there are also responsibilities to patients and thereby to the wider community. Once again, the model does have a social element. The fact that the British Society is also a charity means that it must conform to charity law and show its work has 'public benefit,' or it would lose its status.

The panel's judgement is probably about having a sense of the candidate's authenticity as an analyst, not just their technical skill, as well as an ability to formulate what they do analytically. After all, training analysts are given considerable responsibility in our Society, and they are expected to be able to teach and to be able to communicate their thoughts to students and their peers.

What is it then like to be a training analyst under this system, what are the advantages and disadvantages, and what is it like for the students?

The advantages include the student having an analysis with an experienced analyst, one who has been vetted in some way, however imperfectly but at least rigorously. The Training analysis is usually at relatively low cost – the latter is the deal training analysts informally agree to. If problems arise within the training, for example, because of treating the usually very difficult train-ing patients, this can be immediately looked at within the analysis. Just to give one example from my own experience as a student in the 1970s. My first (female) training patient developed a florid erotic transference to me in the first week of her analysis. As a young student (in my late 20s), I was in a bit of a panic. But I proudly told my analyst in a session that, of course, I myself did not have any erotic feelings towards my patient. My analyst (John Klauber) heard what I said and, after some thought, he said in his inimical, human but slightly amused way, 'We must take this absence of feeling very seriously, Dr Kennedy!'

Of course, he was making an important point about not just cutting off emotions in the analytic encounter but allowing oneself to wonder about them. In the event, my first supervisor, Marion Milner, suggested I make an interpretation about the patient's dependency on me, and the patient's erotic thoughts became much more manageable; they were very much about her early and difficult mothering experience. It was only later that we could look at her adult sexual life.

One could argue that my experience with the patient was an intrusion into the course of my own analysis. I would not see that. I would see this use of the analysis as enhancing my analytic process. It certainly quickly brought up some key issues for me. In addition, what's wrong with the analyst having to manage impingements? Reality is often an impingement. I would suggest it is an idealization of analysis to see the training analyst only providing a 'pure' analysis, free from any external impingement or disruptions. The question is what kind of impingement occurs and how it is managed within an analytic framework.

If the student's personal analysis were outside the institutional setting, one can ask how one may deal with extreme problems both in the analysis and with the candidate's external behaviour? I have heard it said that one could say to the student, 'I can no longer be your Training analyst.' But that is an extreme response and shows how desperate the situation must be. This approach also assumes a remarkable amount of omnipotence in the analyst, as if they know what's best to do. At least in the integrated team approach, one has the benefit of perceptions and views from other colleagues.

The main disadvantage of the BT system is that it may promote undue infantilization, compliance, and conformity in the students, accompanying a powerful transference to the training analyst. This can only add to the sense of the training analysts as a body having enormous power in the Society. This transference may remain an inhibiting factor in institutional relations, sometimes for years. In my experience, it really helps if the training analyst has an ordinary and matter-of-fact attitude to seeing or meeting their old analysands, not too precious an attitude, reducing the inevitable idealization. One also hopes that the analysis itself tackles this idealization directly with the student. One certainly aims to make the training analysis as much a personal analysis as possible, and that does mean keeping the institutional processes in mind, if only to keep to the analytic process. It does mean, however, special attention to maintaining the setting.

Of course, there are many temptations to intervene when you hear of things that go on with, for example, a difficult seminar leader or supervisor. I always regret maintaining analytic neutrality some years ago, when a student was being driven pretty mad by an obsessional supervisor, who was never satisfied with the student and who in turn never wrote reports – luckily the student progress committee eventually intervened. Maybe I should have said something more active to the student about what I thought; I would probably do that now. It might have then helped the student feel they had more authority themselves. These are always complex situations, bordering on the territory of ethics. Leaving the analysis outside the walls of the institution will not eliminate the ethical issues; it just parks them somewhere else.

But in the end, it is also up to the rest of the training structure, as in the original EM, to provide a buffer against the perceived power of the training analyst, by providing the student with the experience of meeting many other analysts and learning about other ways of working.

There may also be a sense that the 'real' analysis can only begin after qualification. I have to say I never actually found this with my own students. I expected it, but the analyses just carried on, albeit with slightly less anxiety about the future. I think if there were indeed such a great difference in the analysis pre and post qualification, then maybe the analysis was anyway on the wrong track.

I do think a downside of the BT is that the lectures and seminars can become too routine and not flexible enough, rather too much like an academic programme rather than a way of facilitating psychoanalytic independence. There is still much to be learned from other ways of managing the curriculum – which too often is designed to keep vested interests happy rather than engaging with the students.

Finally, I would add that one of the main things I valued most from my training experience, apart from my analysis and supervisions, was close friendships with fellow students and young analysts – that included Michael Parsons, Jonathan Sklar, Christopher Bollas, Juliet Mitchell, and others. That sense of camaraderie made the trials and tribulations bearable. We were, of course, siblings in this new psychic home. Some of us have continued to maintain not only friendships but also psychoanalytic dialogues through regular meetings over the years. Our training provided us with a setting for forming these close professional and personal friendships in a way that has helped us bear the stresses and strains of psychoanalytic work, a perhaps unintentional meaning of the word 'formation.'

Notes

1 Klauber (1976, p. 176).
2 Kennedy (2014).
3 Parsons (2014, p. 212ff).
4 Freud (1930, p. 257).
5 Freud (1912, p. 115).
6 Eitingon (1923).
7 Eitingon (1925, p. 305).
8 Makari (2008, p. 373).
9 Balint (1948, p. 170).
10 Makari (2008, p. 373).
11 Freud (1937, p. 247).
12 Freud (1937, p. 248).
13 Freud (1937, p. 249).

8   Loneliness, Solitude, and the Analyst

Introduction – Loneliness/Solitude Dimension

There is a difference between loneliness and solitude, though with some overlap. Loneliness is about being cut off from others, even in their presence. In solitude, one often requires being alone, yet I am by myself with myself in some kind of *internal dialogue*. Since loneliness and solitude are so much a part of the psychoanalyst's work, I shall use the psychoanalytic experience to explore the loneliness/solitude dimension.

Much of the psychoanalyst's development must take place in solitude, which, though rarely absolute, is certainly relative. We may seek support and supervision, continue our own analysis or go back for a while into analysis, discuss cases with colleagues, turn to writing as a way of dealing with the confusion of the work, but in the end we are on our own with patient after patient in the solitude of the consulting room. This solitude can turn into loneliness. While being lonely and having to tolerate loneliness is part of the human condition, there are aspects of the analyst's loneliness that are particular to the analytic setting and to the analyst's identity formation. There are also clinical situations where the patient's own problems with bearing loneliness may well challenge the analyst's capacities.

I will discuss some of the consequences of considering these difficult issues both for the formation of the analyst's identity and in their clinical work, and how such considerations have wider ramifications beyond psychoanalysis.

Various psychoanalytic and other thinkers have tried to make some distinctions between different states of being alone, sometimes between loneliness and solitude, or between different forms of either loneliness or solitude. Though some of these distinctions may be helpful, and I shall emphasize a particular difference between *creative solitude* and a more *passive loneliness*, I think it is difficult to refine these differences, because there is quite an overlap. For example, in the Oxford English Dictionary, Loneliness, with its Middle English origins, refers to the condition of being alone, while Solitude, with its Latin origins, is the state of being alone, being accustomed to aloneness (soleo, I am accustomed) – hardly a distinctive difference, except, as so

DOI: 10.4324/9781003683315-8

often in English, between a word's roots. What might make for a meaningful distinction is to combine the state of the experiencing subject with the quality of their relationship to the other – with, that is, the degree of isolation of the subject. The degree of their solitude may indicate something about their sense of loneliness. The symbolization of absence makes solitude bearable; merely feeling absence without the capacity to speak about it plunges the subject into loneliness.

Overall, loneliness is more like the feeling state of the subject, cut off from others, solitude more the general state of being alone, but with a more secure sense of oneself. As so often in English, the Early English word is closer to basic feeling than the Latin word, which is associated with the more patrician language of invasion – Romans and then Normans. But this may be stretching the difference between the words too much.

Literature on Loneliness and Solitude

Many writers offer descriptions of loneliness, but there are relatively few who tackle the meaning of the term and its various distinctive properties. I have picked out a few who seem to offer particularly valuable insights into the way that different states of loneliness and/or solitude can be distinguished.

Beginning with the psychoanalytic literature, Fromm-Reichmann, in her posthumously published late essay on loneliness,[1] describes the word as containing a basket of terms – culturally determined loneliness, creative loneliness, self-imposed aloneness, compulsory isolation, and real loneliness as seen, for example, in the psychotic patients she treated. She focuses on the severe form of loneliness where there is a deep threat of incommunicable, private emotional experience. This is a disintegrative form of loneliness, which reveals itself in psychotic states, where intimacy is not possible. It renders people who suffer it emotionally paralyzed and helpless; it is associated with extreme states of anxiety. She offers vivid descriptions of psychotic patients' experiences of loneliness, with the implication that an important aspect of therapeutic work with such patients is to help them feel less alone and less ashamed of their loneliness. But of course, such work is massively demanding of the therapist, requiring them to withstand powerful projections and extreme states of anxiety.

Melanie Klein's last paper was 'On the sense of loneliness.'[2] She refers to the inner sense of loneliness that can be there even in company. She suggests that this state is the result of a ubiquitous yearning for an unattainable perfect internal state, linked to the infant's early psychotic anxieties. She links loneliness and the incapacity to sufficiently integrate the good internal object. Loneliness can be diminished by various external factors such as the relation to the parents and appreciation by others, but loneliness can never be eliminated, because the processes which lead to integration are never complete and always involve pain.

Winnicott[3] writes of a sophisticated phenomenon involved in the capacity to be alone, a sign of maturity in emotional development. Instead of focusing on the fear of being alone or the wish to be alone, where the subject withdraws from others, he discussed the positive aspects of the capacity to be alone. The basis for this latter capacity is a secure foundation in early childhood, when the child can enjoy solitary activity such as playing and exploring, knowing that the mother is available as a support, which he describes as being alone in the presence of someone. Once that form of aloneness has been internalized, then there is the possibility of a relaxed form of aloneness. This contrasts with, for example, the hectic and desperate behaviour of the deprived child who is unable to settle to quiet play.

This paper can be fruitfully set beside the Use of an Object paper.[4] 'Object-relating' is described there when the subject is an isolate, functioning at an omnipotent level. Winnicott describes a more mature level of functioning when the subject can use the object or other. The change from relating to using involves a particular process in which the subject destroys the object, but the object survives the destruction. Once the object has survived, the subject can move into a new kind of position where he can start to live a life in a world of alive objects – that is, they are no longer alone and cut off from others, but in live contact with others.

Quinodoz[5] describes how the analyst needs to acquire a well-developed sense of solitude, which involves being able to work through anxieties about object loss and separation, in order to 'tame' the deep anxieties associated with solitude.

Dolto[6] also emphasizes the importance for the young child of periods of secure solitude, where they can explore for themselves, supported by a lively mother who talks to the child. This positive form of solitude is different from isolation, where a child withdraws and may have experienced little positive communication. The former is structuring, peopled by constructive memories; the latter is destructuring, without symbolization.

Buechler[7] is one of the few analysts who specifically tackle the analyst's experience of loneliness. For her, the analyst's loneliness with the patient is affected by (1) the patient's loneliness and potential for collaboration. (2) The patient's diagnostic type. (3) The analyst's stance about countertransference. (4) The other emotions evoked in the analyst by their patient.

She gives vivid clinical descriptions of the analysis of different kinds of patients and how loneliness came into the analysis in various ways, sometimes giving the analyst challenging personal and human dilemmas. She also emphasizes the need for the analyst to bring into the consulting room an 'internal chorus' of identifications to help us deal with these challenges.

There are many literary descriptions of the lonely state of mind, though relatively few that look at the meaning of loneliness. The philosopher and theologian Paul Tillich distinguishes between loneliness as an expression of the pain of being alone, and solitude, which expresses the glory of being alone. The pain of loneliness can be overcome by facing solitude, which for him, like Jesus alone in the desert, means facing the daemonic forces.[8]

In Montaigne's essay on Solitude, man is described as both sociable and unsociable. While we should have a wife, children, goods, and health, that is, a *home*, we must not bind ourselves to them so much that our happiness depends on them. We must 'reserve a back shop all our own, entirely free, in which to establish our real liberty and our principal retreat and solitude.'[9] Thus, the home, though important, needs to have a special space to which one can retreat, but in a creative way.

Solitude is thus the source of strength, provided we know how to use it well. There are dangers in retreating to an ivory tower, but without a safe place to retreat to, we are too dependent upon others. One could add that the analyst's consulting room is a place which provides a mixture of the back shop and the 'front shop.' There is the retreat from the social world, for both analyst and patient, and yet it is at the same time an intense setting for working out dependency issues.

Several writers have expressed the need for what one could call a *creative* solitude, where thoughts can be crystallized, even if the experience can involve much pain and frustration. As Thomas Wolfe describes in his essay on God's Lonely Man, 'if a man is to know the triumphant labour of creation, he must for long periods resign himself to loneliness and suffer loneliness to rob him of the health confidence, the belief and joy which are essential to creative work.'[10] Wolfe cites the *Book of Job* as the most tragic, sublime, and beautiful expression of human loneliness, and as with Job, the joyfulness of love destroys loneliness, providing Wolfe with some comfort against the tragic web of life.

The theme of creative solitude as a necessary feature of the creative process runs implicitly through many writers, from Rousseau's solitary walks and discourses with nature, through the Romantic poets' confrontation with the solitude of landscapes as sources of joy, to modern preoccupations with states of isolation as in Conrad's Heart of Darkness, where Kurtz confronts his truth in the 'great solitude' of the jungle.

Paul Auster describes the way, familiar to many authors, that the writer requires essential solitude in order to write; but he links this to the work required of the reader.

> Every book is an image of solitude, the outcome of a great deal of time spent alone in a room. Literature is at once the product of an author's solitude and a means by which a reader reaches through his own and the author's solitude. In reading, an isolated individual becomes absorbed in something beyond his own preoccupations and communes with another mind.[11]

One might add that the writer needs to have a sense of the reader while he is writing, so that while he is solitary, he needs to reach out to the reader.

There is thus a complex inter-subjective process at work between the solitary writer and the solitary reader, which provides a point of contact for both of them. As Maurice Blanchot put it,

> The work is solitary: this does not mean that it remains uncommunicable, that it has no reader. But whoever reads it enters into the affirmation of the work's solitude, just as he who writes it belongs to the risk of this solitude.[12]

With the literature in mind, I turn now to the specifics of the analytic relationship. I shall develop the distinction between solitude and loneliness but will also explore more of the essential dilemmas about being an analyst in the loneliness of the consulting room.

Loneliness and Solitude for the Psychoanalyst

While on the one hand the psychoanalytic encounter can be intensely engaging for both patient and analyst, can tap into deep, often long-suppressed emotions, can become a source of creativity, and can even on occasions become both life-changing and lifesaving, the encounter can also be very challenging with regard to what has to be endured by both parties for long periods of time. I will here tend to focus on the more challenging aspects of being an analyst, but I do not wish to give the impression that analytic work is predominantly painful and difficult; there are, of course, many times when it is deeply satisfying and indeed is also a privilege to be able to be privy to another's world in such an intimate and engaging way.

One of the most challenging aspects for the analyst is how to come to terms with the psychoanalytic way of life, which imposes certain restraints. Like the writer, we must work on our own, but the analyst has particular pressures to bear. Long periods of necessary isolation must be tolerated, so that the patient's inner life can be given special and focused attention, in a space and setting which is protected from external intrusions. While such protection is necessary for the development of the transference, the concentrated restraint required by the analyst does impact on their own well-being. Indeed, one might say that the analyst has only limited protection from all sorts of 'internal' intrusion into their own mental equilibrium. That is, we cannot leave unscathed from our analytic encounters; there is a price we must pay for doing our work. The increasing focus on using our countertransference, on making creative use of many of these intrusions, adds to the richness of the analytic work, but also adds to the stresses and strains of maintaining the analytic relationship. Tolerating and understanding projections and disturbance, keeping quiet when tempted to speak out, maintaining an analytic stance under the most difficult clinical situations, not to mention standing up for psychoanalysis and for thinking about the unconscious inner life outside the clinical setting when all around us may be avoiding any such thing, all present challenges to our precious and hard-won sense of equilibrium and analytic identity. We may, for example, have stirred up in ourselves powerful memories because of listening to the patient, but we have to keep such memories to ourselves. We have to forego the pleasure of sharing many such intimate experiences evoked by the intensity of analytic listening. In our social life, we often need to refrain from using our analytic techniques to intervene in ordinary relationships, however tempting, otherwise we may undermine defences and create unnecessary antagonism. Yet sometimes the temptation to do a bit of 'wild analysis' is just too much to resist. While occasional use of our skills can be helpful in situations of difficulty or crisis, the temptation to show off our analytic understanding may be driven more by a desperate desire to share our experience rather than maintain our difficult, unusual, and lonely stance.

In order to bear this situation, we have to have a capacity to be alone, but under rather particular circumstances. But that does not take away the reality of the struggle when the analyst must bear the often acute sense of solitude which accompanies analytic work. A certain amount of detachment is necessary to be able to establish and maintain the analytic setting and to make effective decisions about how to intervene, yet that does not eliminate our basic wish for attachment, for relatedness, which we may have to modify considerably.

In order to bear the loneliness of being an analyst, it does seem important for the analyst to be able to have a significant and sustaining life outside the analytic work, even though such work is the core of the analyst's creative life. One can see the dangers of not having a life outside analysis with those analysts who engage in sexual misconduct with one patient. Celenza and Gabbard,[13] in their account of different kinds of boundary violation, point out that this kind of violation typically occurs when the analyst is in the midst of a life crisis such as divorce, illness, or death in the family, where they are cut off from, or cannot use, their usual support networks; they are more lonely than usual. The psychopathology of such analysts varies, but typically they are people who look primarily or even exclusively to professional relationships and activities for sustenance and affirmation of self-worth. Their analytic identity is too much dependent on their professional life. It is as if they cannot bear, at moments of crisis, the pain of being alone with their problems, and, not having a suitable network to turn to, unfortunately use their patient as their comforter. Their paper makes the point that this situation is much more humanly understandable than the boundary violations involving the psychopathic analyst who has no empathy with the patient and shows no remorse for their actions.

Whatever the precise definitions of the terms, the loneliness/solitude dimension is an inevitable accompaniment of the psychoanalytic setting, with the patient on the couch, turned away from the analyst. It is also a feature of those times when we struggle to formulate interpretations, particularly if under pressure from the patient to make sense of some difficult conflict before we are ready. The periods of contact with the patient can be satisfying for both parties, but there are many in-betweens, of silences, uncertainties, periods of desperation and intense moments of loneliness that have to be tolerated, especially with the more ill patients. Indeed, we may be tempted to interpret too much in order to defend oneself against feeling lonely. Listening in silence until one is ready to interpret may be just too much to bear. One of my main points is that being able to deal with these kinds of pressure in a good enough way is related to the gradual development of an *analytic identity*. The analyst's own rootedness in their identity mitigates the trauma of the necessary and inevitable periods of loneliness while doing analysis. One may add that the evidence from Celenza and Gabbard is also that having a secure internal analytic identity is aided by having effective external supports, both from within the analytic community but also from elsewhere.

A psychoanalytic identity takes several years to acquire, and involves a gradual process of development, as a result of repeated and extensive listening to patients analytically over several years. In some ways, this development in the analyst requires something like a 'spiritual' growth, something that goes increasingly inward and, in more depth, and involves an inward transformation.[14] One might add that there is something about the special quality of loneliness in the analytic position which matches what Kierkegaard captures so well – how to express the subject's inwardness, which can be communicated, but indirectly.[15]

Adequate training and analysis are, of course, the basis for the development of an analytic identity. But so is a commitment to undertaking a reasonable amount of analytic work, not that easy these days with all the economic pressures on young analysts. There may also, of course, be institutional reasons that interfere with analytic identity, for example, when an institution can demand too much conformity or, on the contrary, is too chaotic, or split between warring parties. That kind of atmosphere is hardly encouraging to the new analyst.

Whatever the decision about setting up an analytic practice, the path towards a firm analytic identity is never smooth. There are usually a number of fits and starts, with disappointments, knocks to one's narcissism, surprises, traumas, and failures. One has to get used to this lonely kind of work, and sometimes the strain involved in taking so much onto oneself can have the effect on many analysts of being over-concerned with their own contributions and importance. I suspect that this is also a reaction to a number of narcissistic wounds we regularly have to withstand, denigration from the patient being perhaps the easiest to bear. Others less easy to manage include the fallout from unhelpful analytic rivalries within analytic institutions that can at times be very hurtful, as well as the frequent scepticism towards our work shown to us by psychiatric colleagues and the wider public. While Freud often cautioned us to expect resistance to psychoanalysis, reading constant attacks on our work does not exactly help us with our precarious and hard-won sense of analytic identity. But I would suggest that the loneliness of the analyst's work can have an unfortunate side effect, in that there may develop as a reaction formation a tendency to wall oneself off from others in a form of narcissistic character formation, which may manifest itself as an inflated sense of self-importance.

Much of the analyst's development has to take place in solitude, which, though rarely absolute, is certainly relative. As François Dolto put it, in her evocative book on solitude, psychoanalysis is a profession where one is alone. 'Everyone is alone, but the psychoanalyst more so, and there is no one else to whom he can refer because no one else can feel what the analysand subjects him to, even if he can be understood.'[16]

While loneliness and its effects are part of the human condition, the analyst must bear a special kind of loneliness due to their analytic function and the special nature of the analytic relationship. The analytic setting, with the analyst sitting behind the patient, or not providing ordinary social cues in face-to-face meetings, demonstrates literally that the analytic relationship is not an object relationship in the usual sense. That is, on the one hand, the analyst must hold the patient in mind while being unable to express their feelings towards the patient freely; while on the other hand, for the patient, the analyst is enigmatic and frustrating in a way that would be unacceptable in social relationships. With the analyst not being available as a direct object of relationship, then the analytic setting sets in motion a complex search for the human subject, predominantly through contact with the unconscious of both parties. One has to tolerate a good deal of uncertainty, paradox and puzzlement, in addition to the more obvious times when one has to withstand aggression and projection, and deal with the patient's intense longings for more than an analytic relationship, which may, unfortunately, as I have mentioned, lead the vulnerable analyst to act out a boundary violation.

In addition, it is clear that the analyst has a deep need for the patient in order to crystallize their thoughts and to fulfil their own creativity. As I indicated above, there are dangers when this need becomes exclusive. But I also think that we need the patient in other, more private ways, even when one has a good support network outside the analytic framework. I think that the use of what I would call our *private area of suffering* is a vital and therapeutic element of the analytic relationship, a helpful aspect of our countertransference. It is what is inevitably missing in accounts of an analysis, because it will remain silent. I feel that we need to tap into this suffering, a particular area of our subjective experience, the area of the soul. Sometimes, perhaps often, patients are in touch with this area and use it for their own purposes, to avoid conflict, to get us to collude with them, or simply to share their suffering. Thus, our private and lonely sufferings are not only a nuisance, something we hoped our own analysis would have dealt with, but also an inevitable part of the analytic work, which, if used wisely, can be the source of creativity. I think we need to listen to the patient's conscious and unconscious assessment of our private areas of pain and suffering. They may not know what they are reacting to, nor do we have to tell them exactly; but we will hopefully know, provided we do not retain a God-like stance. Our patients reflect back to us our own suffering; they may even wish to protect us from ourselves, which is perhaps particularly seductive and dangerous for the analysis.

It was John Klauber who first asked serious questions about the possible long-term vicissitudes on the analyst of the patient's longings,[17] as well as how analysts deal with the effects of forming relationship after relationship of the deepest and most intimate kind with patient after patient, and the mourning which at some level must be involved for each of them before and after an ending. He asked how the analyst can accommodate themselves to being without the basic cue of human expression, face-to-face contact, for so many hours of the day, and whether it imposes a strain on him, and if so, how this strain can be alleviated. He pointed out that the newly qualified analyst is confronted by object loss on several fronts, losing a variety of supports, and how traumatic this may be, particularly as it will take so long for their analytic role to become integrated into a sustaining sense of analytic identity. Here, one may add that such experience points to a fundamental issue that, as Quinodoz pointed out, what makes the analytic work bearable is being able to tolerate object loss, or, one might add, that absence can be symbolized.

I think one could also add that there are different pressures at various stages of the psychoanalyst's life cycle. The relief and excitement of qualification may help mitigate the early strains of building up an analytic practice. The period between qualifying and becoming an experienced analyst may be particularly difficult when the reality of having to bear hours of analytic listening in the solitude of the consulting room finally hits home. And most difficult of all perhaps is the relinquishing of an analytic practice at the end of one's career, when another form of loneliness hits home, with the loss of the setting and the fear of loss of identity.

The issue of what we mean by identity, let alone a psychoanalytic identity, is a complex one. Having an analytic identity refers to a sense of solidity in one's core identification with psychoanalysis as a theory and practice, an increasing sense of confidence in knowing what one is doing, even when not knowing what is going on in the session. It is probably about finding one's own *voice* as an analyst, being able to develop a particular quality of listening – both listening to the patient's unconscious communications, but also to oneself, with a complex interaction between the two sides. The analytic 'voice' is not only shaped by the clinical encounter, but also by other influences – from training, personal analysis, colleagues, reading, and life.

Clinical Example

There are many times that loneliness may feature in an analysis, but one example may illustrate some of the dilemmas I have touched upon. I shall focus mostly on the transference/countertransference movements.

I am thinking of a man in his 30s, who came into analysis with an acute sense of feeling out of things, not part of the group, cut off from others in a deep way, though able to have his own family. One of the main facts about his presenting history was that he had no recollection before the age of five, when his parents split up. Indeed, much of his early history is still very vague. The mother left his father, taking him and his younger siblings. Before the analysis, my patient had never been told why the father had left, but on asking his mother recently, he had reluctantly told it was because of 'mental cruelty' – though my patient did not find this very convincing. There then began a life of wandering around, and then he went to boarding school from an early age, which he found very difficult. He always felt an outsider, on the margins of the group. It was a very lonely time. He would often walk around the school on his own. This period, the period of extreme loneliness, is remembered by him, and perhaps can be said to have covered over the earlier and even more painful memories of loss.

What he does remember is losing a soft toy, soon after his mother left his father. In compensation, he was taken to a big store and chose a wind-up toy, which he took to boarding school; but this toy was never quite right, never replaced the previous cuddly one.

In analysis, the patient is not that forthcoming with his associations. There are quite a lot of almost 'Harold Pinter-like' pauses. He will say a few lines, wait, and expect me to say something, which I may or may not, depending on whether I have anything to say. He may wait for a long time for me to speak, and I know now that he then begins to feel more and more detached and in a world of his own. So, there is a dilemma about letting the silences go on for too long; it may become counterproductive, as he falls into an extreme sense of loneliness. At the same time, I do not wish to intrude or to be controlled into engaging in a way that means I have all the life. So, there is an issue of the timing of what I say. In the past, I have tried to understand this interaction in various ways. Some relief came from thinking in terms of my becoming in the transference a withholding mother, which seemed to have some link to his own picture of his mother, who has never been particularly warm. However, that relief was short-lived, and the familiar pattern of communication persisted, from time to time leaving both of us in some despair.

At these times, his loneliness can get to me. I feel a mixture of empathy for his plight and irritation at his passivity, which can sometimes leave me feeling cut adrift from my sense of confidence in the analytic process. I then feel lonely, helpless, and disconnected. This is quite different from a more organized sense of solitude, where I can still have an internal dialogue about what is happening. Instead, I don't know what to say, and this can feel quite dismaying. I begin to doubt my analytic identity.

There are times when the atmosphere in the session is particularly detached, flat, and even dead. The issue of deadness and aliveness has often been around – how much he can bear having live contact with me, how much he longs for it and yet also avoids it. Some understanding of this feeling in terms of Green's dead mother complex[18] has been helpful, with the sense of the patient being in the presence of the transference of a depressed or cut off mother, who had once been more alive. This became clearer as I began to understand what was happening as the session was reaching towards its close.

In order to get to that point, I had to re-examine how I had felt intermittently frustrated, controlled, and irritated by his withholding. At these times, I was also aware of his deprivation, the emptiness he has had to cope with since early childhood. He has that mixture common to those with such a childhood – of being like an abandoned child craving for love, but unable to make the kind of live contact which would satisfy him.

What seems to have begun to make a difference to him is trying to differentiate different states of loneliness, and how he feels I am available for him at the beginning of a session and now for about three-quarters of the session – the length of time he can trust in my being available within the session has gradually increased over time. But then, suddenly, I seem to disappear. He will imagine I am elsewhere, particularly if I do not speak much. This can suddenly produce a terrible sense of despair and futility, which may last until the next session. My own experience of these moments in the session itself can be somewhat disorienting. I can feel I am doing my job reasonably well, and then suddenly I doubt myself; I feel alone in the presence of the other, but not in a healthy way. I just feel lonely and cut off. Using this countertransference emotion in order to name the sudden loss of confidence in my presence as the repetition of an early catastrophic loss seems to have made some impact. We finally began to piece together the unbearable depression of his early years when he lost the security of his home life, when the soft toy was lost and replaced with a wind-up toy. The latter may also represent the rather automaton-like nature of his early objects, which become manifest in the transference as his rather controlled way of measuring his associations, at least at times. In addition, one could understand this sense of my being available and then disappearing to him as the repetition of Green's dead mother, the mother who was once available and then no longer. It is as if the nice soft teddy bear, representing the alive mother, becomes replaced by the hard wind-up toy. Whatever the precise nature of the transference constellation, what seemed to bring most relief to the patient was to understand the timing in the session of the sudden states of lonely despair; even to see that these moments had meaning was a relief, that he was not just being abandoned by me, but was in the grip of some unconscious process that we could begin to work out together. He was not totally alone in the presence of an abandoning other.

The Fort/Da Observation and the Loneliness/Solitude Relationship

One could see the fort/da game, already described in Chapter 4, as a kind of description of what takes place regularly in an analysis. With the neurotic patient, there is in the transference a regular kind of coming and going; the analyst is both present and absent for the patient, appears and disappears.

Such transference movements do not create massive anxiety or a great deal of loneliness. However, traumatized and borderline patients bring in an intense way the issue of a going away which feels at times total, with no hope of a return and a traumatic sense of loneliness. And yet they keep coming back to their analysis in the hope that the analytic setting can provide some resolution to their despair. I have suggested that there is always a tension, or strain, between the mother as mere physical object and the mother as an elusive human presence, capable of appearing and disappearing when she wants to, or needs to, whether it is to go to the father or elsewhere, the mother who stirs up the child's yearnings and desires. In the fort/da, one can see the working out of the difference between mother as material object and the mother as an elusive human presence; out of this difference one can see human subjectivity, with all its dilemmas and possibilities, beginning to emerge. The task of the developing child, as well as that of the analytic patient, is, in a sense, to come to the realization that the mother is not a mere physical object, or at least not an object under the child's omnipotent control, but a subject with a mysterious life of her own, relating to other subjects, the father and others. The dawning of this realization is never easy; there is always a certain amount of strain involved in the process of coming to terms with the mother's elusiveness, more so when the mother's absence is prolonged, or her return highly problematic.

It is hard to forget the context of the fort/da observation, aspects of which haunt it and give it particular and poignant significance. It is placed early in his book *Beyond the Pleasure Principle,* following on what Freud describes as the 'dark and dismal subject of the traumatic neurosis.'[19] From the terrors of the repetition of war memories, he moves to the apparently lighter topic of children's play, but which reveals a young child coming to terms with the mother's temporary absence. And yet within a short time, as a footnote tells us, as if in passing, we learn that this mother (in fact, Freud's beloved daughter Sophie) died some four years after the observation, before Freud wrote his book. One can thus see the observation in a more primeval light; a mother dies and is then resurrected in the text. Furthermore, though we are also told that he had been jealous of a younger brother, we are not told that this brother, Heinz, also died from TB sometime after his mother. This child's death, according to Ernest Jones, produced 'the only occasion in his life when Freud was known to shed tears.'[20] The loss, no doubt coming after his daughter's death and the emergence of his cancer of the jaw, was almost unbearable and produced in him symptoms of depression.

There are also other personal references surrounding Freud's focus on the child of a year and a half, for this was about the age he was when his younger brother, Julius, died. This death was to haunt Freud; he admitted that the evil wishes he had against this early arrival had aroused self-reproaches, which continued to affect his personal relationships. For example, he would link his fainting fits around the time of the increasing tensions with Jung to the effect on him of his younger brother's death. One may finally note that around the

age of 18 months was the time when the Wolf Man was likely to have wit-
nessed the primal scene.[21] Thus, the significance of the fort/da observation is
multi-determined, linking the personal and the theoretical, real traumas in
Freud's life to general considerations of the nature of trauma.

In *Beyond the Pleasure Principle*, Freud notes how dreams in traumatic
neurosis bring the patient back into the situation of the accident or 'fright,' a
situation from which he wakes up in 'another fright.'[22] From the appearance
and reappearance of the traumatic situation in the dream, he leads onto the
appearance and reappearance of the mother in the world of the young child,
a situation which, though apparently lighter, is fraught, as we have seen, with
dark resonances of traumatic elements in Freud's personal life. From the fort/
da, Freud moves onto the analytic patient and then to how the mental apparatus tries to protect itself from traumatic stimuli by means of a protective
shield.

In Freud's original observation, one can see the fort/da game as a positive
use of repetition. The game helped the child to cope with the mother's comings and goings, as well as providing a means, according to Lacan, of becoming inserted into the Symbolic Order and into language. In the space between
these comings and goings, the child was able to find a place to play; there
was a space for representation. The child could let go of the mother once he
had found a repetitive but symbolic means of representing her leaving him.
This positive use of repetition contrasts with a more compulsive and insistent quality of repetition which has a more mindless, or 'daemonic,' quality,
related to the power of the unconscious repressed. One could imagine a
delicate balance between these two kinds of repetition, depending on the
time for waiting for the mother's return, what state she was in when she left,
what state the child was in when she left, and what state both are in on her
return. Of course, the fort/da game occurs without the mother, and yet there
are many occasions when something similar takes place in the presence of
the mother. Various kinds of comings and goings occur in the complex interactions between mother and child, as I have described in Chapter 4.

Further Thoughts on Loneliness and Solitude

Both Klein and Fromm-Reichmann approached the topic of loneliness at the
end of their careers; indeed, in both cases, these were their last papers. For
Klein, loneliness was an inevitable state of mind, indicative of the fact that
integration is never fully achievable. While one may mitigate the feeling of
loneliness, it is not something that we can avoid. There is certainly a sense in
this paper here of an analyst at the end of their life looking into the void, of
having to face the pathos and pain of approaching death. There is something
of that quality in the late work of great artists. Edward Said[23] in his poignantly
last and unfinished book approaches the issue of 'late style' in such artists. For
example, he suggests that there is something in late Beethoven, as in his late
quartets, that remains unreconciled and fragmentary; they acutely express

a sense of abandonment, in contrast to the relentless quality of his second period works, such as the Fifth Symphony. Indeed, one might add that in his last works, he pushes harmony and form to the limit, moving away from the 'home' key at times so that one may wonder if home will ever be reached; there are even moments, as in his last piano sonata, when time itself seems suspended. The prerogative of such late style is that it

> …has the power to render disenchantment and pleasure without resolving the contradiction between them. What holds them in tension, as equal forces straining in opposite directions, is the artist's mature subjectivity, stripped of hubris and pomposity, unashamed either of its fallibility or of the modest assurance it has gained as a result of age and exile.[24]

Anthony Storr, in his book *Solitude*,[25] also discusses late Beethoven as an exemplar of the late or third period in an artist's development. The last quartets, for example, are less concerned with communication, are unconventional in form, display an absence of rhetoric, and explore remote areas of experience. Such work is deeply expressive of deep inward experience, very much the theme of last works.

One may suppose that as a result of the artist achieving a point in their life where their identity is firm enough to be able to face their own dissolution, these last works convey in their form and expression what is unattainable; that human happiness, while achievable in brief moments, cannot last, though the yearning for it may persist. Faced by approaching death, the artist, or indeed analyst, becomes ever aware that happiness and integration are transient, loneliness in some form inevitable.

One may infer from these considerations that solitude as an active state of mind, as opposed to the more passive experience of experiencing loneliness, can be creative under certain conditions. The kind of creativity shown in the last works referred to represents some of the highest human achievements, where solitude before death becomes the source of illumination. But even long before death, solitude can be facilitated by encouraging deep contact with one's inner world, or what I would describe as the depths of the soul. This contrasts with much of contemporary Western culture, with its constant bombardment of the senses, the continuous call of the mobile and the ever-present text message, which at times appear as manic defences against any possibility of imagining oneself alone. Storr[26] also points out how solitude can encourage the growth of the imagination, so long as it is not too extreme. Indeed, it does seem that imaginative capacity tends to become particularly highly developed in gifted individuals who, for one reason or another, have passed rather solitary childhoods. The point made is that, provided the childhood circumstances are not so severe as to cause lasting and profound damage, a certain amount of solitariness can encourage the imagination to flourish. Though, of course, one may add that with a number of creative artists who

have experienced childhood loneliness, their subsequent personal relationships may well have suffered. Storr cites as examples of these kinds of artists
Kipling, Saki, and P.G. Wodehouse, all of whom had the experience of being
farmed out as children, without the experience of a secure childhood home.
As a result, all three suffered from difficulties in forming close relationships.

In the analytic setting, one may tend to focus more on the relationship
difficulties than on the creative imagination. Yet we also touch on at least
the roots of imagination, or when it can become blocked. Bearing loneliness
seems to me an essential aspect both of being an analyst and of some analytic
work, particularly with patients who have spent periods of their childhood in
extreme states of isolation. Helping them to manage their isolation and reach
a point of creative solitude may be very important for them. In the main clinical example, the patient reached a point where there was some confidence
that he could face the prospect of my absence.

Having confidence in the return of a loved one seems essential to the
capacity to bear loneliness, even in adversity. I want to finish with a quotation from Dietrich Bonhoeffer's last letter from prison to his friend Eberhard
Bethge before he was taken to a concentration camp, as an example of how
even under extreme situations, such love can be sustaining.

> These will be quiet days in our homes. But I have had the experience
> over and over again that the quieter it is around me, the clearer do I feel
> a connection to you. It as though in solitude the soul develops senses
> we hardly know in everyday life. Therefore I have not felt lonely or
> abandoned for one moment. You, the parents, all of you, the friends and
> students of mine at the front, all are constantly present to me…Therefore
> you must not think that I am unhappy. What is happiness and unhappi-
> ness? It depends so little on the circumstances; it depends really only on
> that which happens inside a person.[27]

Notes

1   Fromm-Reichmann (1990).
2   Klein (1963).
3   Winnicott (1958).
4   Winnicott (1969).
5   Quinodoz (1993, 1996).
6   Dolto (1994).
7   Buechler (1998).
8   Tillich (1963, p. 5).
9   Montaigne (1580, p. 214).
10 Wolfe (1941, p. 146).
11 Auster (1982, p. 136).
12 Blanchot (1955, p. 22).
13 Celenza and Gabbard (2003).
14 Parsons (2006).
15 Kierkegaard (1941).
16 Dolto (1994, p. 151).

17　Klauber (1976).
18　Green (1983).
19　Freud (1920, p. 14).
20　Jones (1961, p. 550).
21　Freud (1918, p. 37).
22　Freud (1920, p. 13).
23　Said (2006).
24　Said (2006, p. 148).
25　Storr (1988, p. 174).
26　Storr (1988, p. 106ff).
27　Bonheoffer (1970, p. 419).

9 Some Psychoanalytic Thoughts about Incest

Most psychoanalytic theories of development emphasize the need for the young child to be able to have an early experience of safe dependence, safe physical and emotional boundaries around them, and help to be able to tolerate inevitable environmental frustrations. Fundamental to this sense of security is the sense that the family home is a place free from major intrusions and disruptions. As described previously, I have put forward the notion of a 'Psychic Home' as a significant element of our sense of identity.[1] The psychic home provides an organizing structure for the sense of emerging identity; it is built up from a number of different elements, as with the physical home, which forms its substrate. There are intrapsychic elements as well as intersubjective elements involving the social world, identifications, and relationships. The sense of home as the ground of our being, the place we need to feel secure, is fundamental.

One may then ask what happens to the mind's development when these conditions are not provided, when bodily boundaries are intruded upon, and when primitive sexual desires are enacted in the real world, when the home becomes a place of terror and abuse instead of safety and security.

Incest is forbidden in all human societies

> because it brings together persons that are considered to be 'too alike'; they share essential components of their being, whether these be physical – sperm, blood, milk, or flesh - or immaterial, the soul, or the name. Bringing these components into contact through sexual intercourse is forbidden because this excessive sameness can be detrimental to them and those close to them. But it can also be detrimental to the reproduction of the social order as a whole.[2]

Incest 'destroys the responsibility and protection that family members owe each other in order to sustain their social ties and maintain social and personal equilibrium.'[3]

The incest taboo implies a certain amount of inhibition of sexual desire in order for humans to live in society. Those who commit incestuous acts do so consciously to satisfy their desires and are seeking pleasure and domination,

DOI: 10.4324/9781003683315-9

while also being aware that it is forbidden. And so, there is a pleasure in transgression. The writings of de Sade illustrate the pleasure associated with this transgression. Chasseguet-Smirgel describes how the pleasure in transgression in de Sade is sustained by the fantasy that

> in breaking down the barriers which separate man from a woman, child from adult, mother from son, daughter from father, brother from sister, the erotogenic zones from each other, and in the case of murder, the molecules in the body from each other – it has destroyed reality, therefore creating a new one.[4]

She calls this the 'anal universe,' where all differences are abolished, and chaos prevails.

For the victims who have been forced to be seduced by the abuser at the receiving end of this chaos, there is considerable damage to their sense of identity.

The word incest comes loaded with considerable horror, and one cannot minimize this understandable reaction. But to understand and help those who have been abused in this way, I prefer to emphasize that incest is usually sexual abuse within the family home, and that home is often highly dysfunctional. Such incest both produces mental disturbance and is also the result of such disturbance within one or more family members.

To give a flavour of the kind of families where such incestuous abuse can occur, I saw a family in court proceedings some time ago. Social services had been alerted by a member of the community to grave concerns about the family, with the children being physically and emotionally harmed by the father, and possibly also the girls being sexually abused. Once the investigation was started, the mother took an older girl and a boy with her, while her youngest, 'Sally,' was taken into foster care. Another child, a late teenager, chose to remain with the father. From reading the documents and my various interviews with the family, it was clear that the father had exerted a sadistic control over the family, terrorizing them and preventing contact with the outside world, including schools. I was amazed to discover that the children had had hardly any formal education, despite being bright, and that the educational authorities had never picked this up. When seen by professionals soon after leaving the home, the mother appeared rather confused and helpless at times, glad to be away from the control of the husband but appearing vulnerable and uncertain about herself. There remained doubts about whether she could remain separate from her husband. By the time I saw her, she had begun to become more independent and to begin to live a normal life for the first time in years. What became clear was that she and the children had been victims of the most severe emotional and physical battering, and as a result, they had been deeply traumatized.

The mother described in detail the kind of life they lived until she managed to escape from the home. There was independent evidence of these assertions and backing from her children. She said that the father made constant inappropriate sexual comments about the children, even when they were small. For example, in his grooming actions, he would comment on Sally's small breasts, saying that they would soon be bigger and sexier, and so on.

The mother's own position in the family was eroded over the years so that she was marginalized, as if he were hoping she would simply disappear. She would often get beaten up on the upper arms, so the bruises would not show. He gave that up after a while but then started various mind games, for example, denying food to them and playing one person off against another in the family. He would beat up whoever was in his way and use the oldest child as his spy. The two of them would listen behind doors. If the mother had said a word out of place, he would be violent, smashing up crockery or furniture, for instance. The father controlled what they watched on television. The mother was not allowed to have the house keys. The house was not in her name. There were never any locks on the doors in the house so that he could also enter any room he wanted. As the older boy became more independent, the situation deteriorated and he became a target of the father's hate, denying him food until at last he ran away, staying with friends.

When I interviewed Sally, she was clearly bright but deeply traumatized. It was difficult to get her to speak in detail about what had happened. But she admitted that her father would show them, including herself, sick pornographic films. She explained that the father wanted Sally to watch them in order to prime her up for sex with him later. Clearly, the older child had already been sexually abused, as came out in due course, and it was normalized for her. It was clear that the father was a very perverted man, who had used the most extraordinary control over the family. One does not often see such an extremely dysfunctional family without the authorities intervening much earlier. In the end, the children were, of course, removed from his care. He was not allowed to have contact, but the older child, who was beyond the age of consent, chose to live with him. Meanwhile, the mother was able to be rehabilitated, was back with all her children except the oldest girl, and lived satisfactorily away from the father.

There are special situations where adults may commit incest with other adults, such as when adopted children and their natural parents or siblings seek each other out and meet up. As Betty Lifton described,[5] the sexual attraction that adoptees may feel to the biological parent or sibling and the parent or sibling to the child is one where idealization predominates. With a reduced sense of the role of the incest taboo because of not living together closely, in this illusory world, 'incestuous feelings, consummated or not, are an attempt to undo the damage of rejection that the adopted baby felt when it went into exile. Merging with either birth parent or sibling is like returning home.'[6] The need is for reconnection, which becomes sexualized. The outcome of consummated encounters, as in Sophocles' Oedipus Tyrannus, is usually bad, as incest cannot satisfy an adoptee's insatiable emotional need. If the adopted family can provide for the adoptee secure attachments, then presumably the risks of subsequent incest are minimized.

Returning to incest within the family home, the abused mind of the child seems to show varying degrees of damage and developmental distortion, depending on the nature of the abuse, the quality of family relationships in the home, and the resilience of the child. In later life, the abused adult inevitably brings with them feelings of abandonment, mistrust, and parental failure, which are repeated in a psychoanalysis, with varying degrees of intensity, depending on how the original trauma has been dealt with. Having been used as mere objects to satisfy primitive sexual and/or aggressive impulses in adults, they themselves in adult life show varying degrees of psychic damage, particularly in their capacity for self-reflection. They may never feel that they have a secure psychic home, one free from the terror of suffering.

Ferenczi, because of the psychoanalysis of abused adults, had described in his 1933 paper 'Confusion of Tongues Between Adults and the Child'[7] the traumatic impact on children of being exposed to adult sexuality. He described how incestuous seductions may lead to the child feeling physically and morally helpless, that their personalities are not sufficiently consolidated in order to be able to protest, for the overpowering force and authority of the adult makes them speechless.

> The same anxiety, however, if it reaches a certain maximum, compels them to subordinate themselves like automata to the will of the aggressor, to divine each one of his desires and to gratify these; completely oblivious of themselves, they identity themselves with the aggressor.[8]

The aggressor becomes internalized into a kind of internal abuser of the child's developing mind, a foreign and malignant introject. Ferenczi describes how 'the most important change in the psyche of the child by the anxiety-fear-ridden identification with the adult partner is *the introjection of the guilt feelings of the adult* which makes hitherto harmless play appear as a punishable offence.'[9]

If the sexual trauma is too great or is repeated, then the child develops splits in the personality, and it may become difficult to maintain contact with the fragments without confusion, each fragment behaving like a separate personality unaware of the existence of the others, which Ferenczi describes as *atomization*.

Ferenczi came to these conclusions by examining the nature of the analytic relationship in certain traumatized patients, where he noted moments of extreme anxiety: the patients accusing him of insensitivity, expressing rage towards him, while at the same time, the patients were mostly compliant and overly willing to accept his interpretations. He was also aware of his own countertransference feelings of hatred towards the patients at times, which he linked to what the patients as children probably experienced from the traumatizing adult.

Ferenczi made the point with brutal honesty that the analyst in these situations was bound to make mistakes; they come with the territory. But to help the patient, it is important for the analyst to admit mistakes, to honestly endeavour to avoid them in the future, in order to create confidence in the analyst.

> *It is this confidence that establishes the contrast between the present and the unbearable traumatogenic past,* the contrast which is absolutely necessary for the patient in order to enable him to re-experience the past no longer as hallucinatory reproduction but as an objective memory.[10]

In a sense, the analytic experience provides a setting for the possibility of just such a resolution of past abuse. Indeed, the analysis of the abused adult is perhaps less concerned with the issues of recovered memories of the past as such than with confronting the emotional impact of their abuse, and the effect of the abuse on their mind's emotional functioning. Not infrequently, this issue arises in the analysis when the patient makes a particular kind of emotional impact on the analyst, as Ferenczi first described. I think it would be too simplistic to describe the situation as being one in which the analyst becomes the abuser in the transference; though not untrue, this seems to me too gross a description of what may take place. Rather, the analyst almost inevitably proves to be a failure; there is a breakdown in their usual functioning – a failure of nerve or some lapse in concentration. The reasonably empathic atmosphere may suddenly deteriorate, with the ready creation of misunderstandings, which may leave the analyst feeling they have somehow mistreated the patient. The abused adult will recreate the emotionally absent parent, the parent who could not bear their child's pain and vulnerability, and who has left the child with a sense that the environment has fundamentally failed them and that there is a kind of breach, or unbridgeable gap, in their parenting experience. An unbridgeable gulf may suddenly appear between patient and analyst, which either party may be tempted to deal with by some kind of precipitous action, such as termination. Sexualization of the transference, or an erotic transference, may or may not become a feature of the analysis for a while, but it is not inevitable. *Bearing the unbearable* is an issue in any analysis, but with the abused adult it somehow becomes acutely relevant. Other themes may include the familiar one of testing the analytic boundaries and great anxiety about trusting the analyst. The patient may wish to seduce the analyst into over-emphasizing the role of the abuse by, for example, tapping into the analyst's wish to find answers rather than accept uncertainty. Finally, the pre-abused child's body may become idealized, while the post-abused body may become a source of persecution. The patient's body, which obviously experienced real intrusion and damage, may feel unintegrated.

There is now considerable evidence from clinical and research findings[11] to show that sexual abuse, usually involving genital and/or anal penetration, has lasting effects on the child's developing mind and personality, including the production of wide-ranging behavioural, emotional and learning difficulties. Psychosomatic symptoms, over-preoccupation with sexual matters, inappropriate sexual behaviour, and aggressive behaviour, can occur in those severely and persistently abused. In adolescence, sexual abuse can be associated with anorexia, attempted suicide, self-harm, prostitution and long-term depression. Increasing evidence of previously undisclosed sexual abuse is being discovered in the population of psychiatric patients. I have seen several women who seemed normal until the birth of their first child, when memories of their own child abuse suddenly flooded them, once they were faced with the reality of their own vulnerable child.

Those who have experienced sexual abuse within the family show the typical features of sexual trauma, though there seem to be some features that can be discerned. Brandon MacCarthy, a pioneer in the psychoanalytic treatment of sexually abused patients, points out how much *loss* is central to the dynamic of such abuse.[12] For example, he noted with father-daughter incest that prior to the first sexual encounter there has often been a significant loss, such as the break-up with a partner or a major family bereavement, notably the death of the perpetrator's mother. 'It is as though the experience of such losses mobilizes a need to seek restitution by reasserting earlier rights to intimacy over the child, in an attempt to undo the loss.'[13] If the incestuous act begins within the first five years, the child seldom has a clear memory or understanding of what took place, but this may well result in confusion about body parts and boundaries.

Secrecy within the family is common when incest occurs; sometimes as Estela Welldon describes, the 'secret' of incest has been hidden for years.[14] There are those in the know in the family and those who don't want to know, such as a parent who keeps silent about their partner's abusive actions and collude with the attack on the child through depression, fear, or merely denial. There is increased risk of incest by turning to a child for comfort when a couple fail to communicate or cannot provide emotional support to one another. The seduction may be rationalized by the often unemphatic parent as a need for warmth, or to 'keep sex in the family,' or to 'keep the family together.' Sometimes the daughter unconsciously colludes in father/daughter incest, 'not only because of her father's demands but because she is responding to her mother's inability to cope, and may even feel betrayed if sexual attentions pass to another sibling.[15] But the burden of secrecy and accompanying feelings of shame and guilt may become too great for a child to live with, and may lead to the outbreak of behavioural or emotional disorders, with a split between affectionate and sexual currents of feeling.'

Mothers who commit incest, as described by Welldon, do not allow their children to develop their own sense of individuality.[16] Such acts are the equivalent in women of a perversion, with the dehumanization of the other through the use of power and by means of sexual gratification.

Welldon also shows how incest operates on a number of different levels simultaneously, with a discharge of tension between the parents, sexual gratification where the child is available to be secretly seduced, and where this secrecy, essential to the incest dynamic, may include a degree of special recognition and favour with the family for that particular child, and also with the discharge of aggression and hostility towards the other partner, which the child then receives as a kind of substitute.

I do want to emphasize the need to be cautious in making assertions about the status of memories of abuse. The diagnosis of sexual abuse in children is a complex affair, involving detailed assessment of the child's reports of abuse, combined with attention to the nature of the family pathology and the nature of any corroborative evidence, while recognizing the frequent presence of coercion of children by adults, with threats to the children if the abuse is revealed. Memories of abuse recovered in adult analysis cannot be subjected to the same clear procedures, and they are thus inevitably subject to considerable doubt. The analyst also needs to be wary of a kind of unconscious coercion on their part, either to suggest abusing memories or to help to deny them. I would suggest:

- that such recovered memories be subjected to a rigorous examination of their supposed reality by, for example, the analyst remaining initially sceptical about their reality;
- that the memories need to be put in the context of the analytic process, the whole shape of the analysis, and the nature of other memories of the past, as well as the quality of the transference at the time of their recall;
- and that the analyst is cautious about accepting the reality of the abuse, however convincing at first it may appear.

It is worth noting in this context that in his early paper on the aetiology of hysteria, Freud[17] draws up comprehensive criteria for assessing the reality of infantile sexual scenes. These criteria include:

- the uniformity which they exhibit in certain details;
- the initial insignificance which the patient first of all ascribes to the events, despite their horrifying consequences;
- the way the patient does not put particular stress on the events;
- and, finally, the relationship of the scenes to the content of the whole of the rest of the case history.

Freud compares the unravelling of the early scenes of seduction with the putting together of a child's picture puzzle. Having subjected the memories to a rigorous examination, it may then be possible to accept the abuse as having happened. Indeed, it may be very important, for clinical and human reasons, for the patient to feel that the analyst has understood that there has been real abuse in the patient's past, that it can be dealt with and talked about, but that one does not necessarily have to accept that the abuse explains everything. We cannot, of course, expect absolute certainty in this area, for the evidence involved in the analytic process is not of the kind involved in the natural sciences; but more like that involved in the social and legal field, where life has to be lived and decisions made on everyday criteria. Thus, if natural-science evidence were used in cases of child abuse, probably no child would be protected from an abuser. Freud began by believing that hysteria was primarily caused by the sexual molestation of children. As is well known, he then felt that he had overvalued reality and undervalued fantasy.[18] I would suggest that we overvalue neither reality nor fantasy; but that we accept that there is a complex interweaving of both fantasy and reality in the processes of memory. Though this interweaving process may complicate judgments about the reality of past events, it also provides for the richness and complexity of the analytic task and makes it one particularly well suited to explore the nature of memory.

I will now present some disguised *clinical material* from a 30-year-old woman in analysis, who had experienced sexual abuse as a child from a close male family member. The memories of abuse were repressed until quite early in the analysis, when she got into a difficult work relationship. She would constantly complain about a man at work who was mistreating her, and so on. This was someone on whom she had pinned great hopes, and his treatment of her was a great disappointment to her. Of course, at first, I assumed this was all very relevant transference material and took it up in this way. However, my doing so made little difference to her sense of being misused, and, in her own words, abused.

From what I knew of her family background, there were indications of some parental failure. She had had some basic good experiences, but the parents had tended to leave her and her sibling in the care of relatives from time to time. The fact that she was left in my care in the analysis, that she felt abused at work, that she had a certain amount of difficulty in dealing with fantasy and dreams that she was also rather controlling of me in sessions, and that there had been significant gaps in her parenting, made me suspect some kind of childhood abuse.

Eventually, and rather tentatively, I wondered with her if she had been molested in some way as a child. My question produced some relief, and, soon after, memories of sexual abuse by a male member of the close family, which she had kept to herself as a child and then forgotten. Her sense of grievance towards the work-figure retreated. I should also add that she has never wanted to seek revenge, either on her abuser or her parents, for what had happened, as has been the case with some patients undergoing various kinds of therapy. Nor has the abuse become the major focus of the analysis. There are many other issues, but it does remain highly significant as an event around which crystallized so much of her emotional life; and it does convince me, after careful consideration, that the abuse had occurred.

After her recall of abuse, I became rather idealized for a while in the analysis for having understood her. It took some time before she could really show her disappointment with me. But breaks were very difficult, with intense feelings of loss and abandonment. There were, for a time, very fragmented sessions, with intense psychotic anxieties predominating. I then seemed to become the detached mother, unable to relate affectively to the child: the mother who could not pick up that she was going to leave her child in unsafe hands in her absence.

For obvious reasons of confidentiality, it would not be appropriate to set out too much more of her history; but I shall instead present part of a session which I think highlights some of the issues around her need to make an emotional impact on me.

The background to this mid-week session, a month or so before a Christmas break, was that I had had to change the previous day's session time, several weeks before. She had been unusually and exceedingly furious with me as the day of the different-time session approached.

She began with a *dream*.

I had moved my consulting room. The new place was attached to the American embassy. [America is often a reference to me, because of my name.] She came to see me a little before time. She sat outside on a ledge, comfortably. I came out and said that she could not wait there. There was a fierce argument between us. I accused her of intruding. I was unreasonable and wanted her to go. She was disgusted and upset.

In the session, she soon became furious with me again, as she had to submit to me. She complained that patients must adapt to analysts, and not the other way round. I first said that perhaps she was furious with me for appearing to put myself first and not think about her and what she might feel about the session change. Still with some fury and sense of grievance, she said that what I said reminded her of how she had to adapt to her parents: how they went off, leaving her in her uncle's unsafe care. She expressed a deep sense of grievance about what had been done to her. Also, she felt second-class. She had had to be too responsible as a child, when she was not ready for it. I was struck by the feelings she described of being a helpless child and her attitude to the changed time of the session, and how she talked about having to be in my care on what she felt were my terms, not under her control. I said it sounded as if the time change had made her feel powerless and passive about what had been done to her. And I added that she sounded afraid of what her anger might have done to me.

This led to various childhood memories, revolving around the theme of how her parents could not tolerate her anger. I took up the feelings of despair that she had not been allowed to have, that had arisen around the session change, and which she was able to show me. Later, we touched on the way that she felt we were no longer in touch when she had felt I had thrown her out and abandoned her. The subsequent session highlighted how her mother had had difficulties tolerating signs of protest from my patient, perhaps part of the reason why my patient kept the abuse to herself. This issue had left my patient with difficulties about being able to tolerate dependency in herself and those close to her. She tended to use control to fend off feelings of chaos when she became intimate with another person. She was also surprised she could be so angry with me, and yet fond of me. This mixture of feelings was a new experience for her. I did feel that something quite important had taken place, in that an essential element – that the parenting failure that had allowed the abuse to take place and to be kept secret – had been repeated in the transference to me, giving the opportunity for some working-through of the trauma.

She had tried to provoke me with her fury. I had to restrain myself from getting into an argument, or from trying to persuade her that she was being unreasonable in being so angry about a minor session change, one which had been anticipated some weeks before. Her unusually fierce anger had certainly made its impact in the session before the one I have reported, in which I had been unable to say very much. I was just aware of needing to hold on and not be provoked too much. I did spend some time after that session wondering what it was about, which helped me cope when I saw her again.

I think a major anxiety in the session I have reported was a fear of abandonment. My patient had to make an impact on me about this issue, and I had to feel the full brunt of her fury. Failure to do so, including, perhaps, a premature interpretation of it, might have resulted in a different kind of failure, which would not have addressed the central issue of the way she had never been allowed to have her emotions, or the way they had not been suitably registered and tolerated. The trauma of abuse, with bodily intrusion, had taken place in a particular emotional context, and it was this context, which was important to clarify, as much as the actual abuse itself.

There is also the issue of the attack on the vulnerable and dependent child by the adult perpetrator. Destructive attacks on children can, unfortunately, have quite specific meaning for the adult perpetrator. The abused child, at a particular moment of vulnerability – for example, when they show acute signs of distress or helplessness, or when they show signs of temper and separateness from the parents' control – can be suddenly experienced by the parent as an enormous threat. The psychic pain shown by the helpless or out-of-control child cannot be tolerated by the abusing parent. In severe cases, the child can be seen as all-destructive and as taking away the parent's goodness. The parent cannot experience the pain of the helpless child as it poses too great a threat to the parent's self, which has great difficulty in being able to reflect on experiences.

There may also be a vengeful aspect to the attack, whether it be physical and/or sexual. The damage done to the child is a revenge for the psychic and physical damage done to the parents, or other perpetrator, when they themselves were children. The cruelty or malignancy sometimes shown by the abusing parent to their victim seems to be, in part, a result of the unconscious need to have revenge for the neglected child in themselves.

Treatment of the abused adult may involve having to deal with various 'abuse-equivalents.' There is the repetition in the transference of the kind of parental-care system around the child which led to the abuse. The abused child has been subjected to significant impingements, with breaks in the provision of continuous care. These gaps in the holding structure and in the sense of a stable and intact psychic home may be small enough to be glossed over, or to be kept just about intact by some kind of temporary repair. Or the gaps in the holding structure may be great enough to cause major psychic damage, with borderline pathology. In treatment, the analyst may be seen as part of a constantly failing environment. There may also be a wish to keep the analyst under total control, for example, through the fantasy of merging. The analyst may experience their own mind being abused by the patient's wish to merge with it and to take it over. Any sign of independence shown by the analyst, for example, by making interpretations, may be sorely resented by the patient, which again makes treatment of the severely abused adult challenging at times, as Ferenczi pointed out.

Notes

 1 Kennedy (2014).
 2 Godelier (2004, p. 3).
 3 Godelier (2004, p. 52).
 4 Chasseguet-Smirgel (1985, p. 3).
 5 Lifton (1994, pp. 225–240).
 6 Lifton (1994, p. 239).
 7 Ferenczi (1933).
 8 Ferenczi (1933, pp. 298–299).
 9 Ferenczi (1933, p. 299).
10 Ferenczi (1933, p. 296).
11 Bentovim et al. (1988).
12 Macarthy (2005).
13 Macarthy (2005, p. 115).
14 Welldon (1998).
15 Welldon (1998, p. 133).
16 Welldon (1998, p. 98ff).
17 Freud (1896, p. 205).
18 Freud (1896, p. 204, fn.).

10 Struggling with Words

Aspects of the Psychoanalysis of a Borderline Man

I will describe, by means of detailed clinical material, part of the analysis of a borderline man, whom I shall call Mr X, concentrating on the great struggle he had in using words in the analytic relationship, which led to feelings of confusion in both me and him, and made it difficult to foster significant change.

I will focus on an intense way that Mr X related to me, in which there was a wish to merge with and become one with me, a situation similar in some respects to certain aspects of the relation between mother and baby. Glasser, among others, has described this way of relating as a major component of what he calls the 'core complex.'. This component is a 'deep-seated and pervasive longing for an intense and most intimate closeness to another person, amounting to a "merging," or "state of oneness," a "blissful union."'[1]

Accompanying the wish to merge with the analyst, there often seems to be in the patient a wish to confuse the analyst. That is, while there may be a wish for blissful union and 'fusion,' what actually takes place is a mix-up of patient and analyst, so that it is difficult for the patient to differentiate himself from the analyst; and there is then what one might call a situation of 'loose identifications.' In clinical terms, this may mean that it is particularly hard to sort out maternal and paternal elements from the transference, which may lead to both patient and analyst feeling confused or at a loss. In addition, the merging component may be accompanied by an acute ability by the patient to penetrate the analyst's mind, perhaps by a process akin to projective identification, which may make the analyst feel intruded upon and uncomfortable. Even if the patient cannot really succeed in penetrating the analyst's mind, the patient may be excessively concerned about what is going on in the analyst's mind. If this is the case, the patient may then find it difficult to think about his own mind and to have coherent thoughts, while the analyst is left at such times feeling as if he were the only one in the room who can think coherently.

In a certain number of borderline patients, including Mr X, one may construct from their adult sexual life the prior existence of what one could call 'Primary Erotic Care,' i.e., what in effect Freud outlined in his Leonardo study as an intensely intimate and erotically tinged relationship between mother and baby. This situation would seem to be, as it were, the price that we all

DOI: 10.4324/9781003683315-10

pay for the existence of the intense bond between mother and child. As Freud wrote,

> A mother's love for the infant she suckles and cares for is something far more profound than her later affection for the growing child. It is in the nature of a completely satisfying love-relation, which not only fulfils every mental wish but also every physical need; and it represents one of the forms of attainable human happiness, that is not little measure due to the possibility it offers of satisfying, without reproach, wishful impulses which have long been repressed.[2]

In addition to the intense relation to the mother, there is often, as Freud also pointed out in the Leonardo study, the child's awareness of the father's absence. In Leonardo's case, the father was physically absent, but also, and what was important in determining his object relations, the father was psychically absent, i.e., there was an actively felt absence.

I would also suggest that the urge for intimate closeness with the object is somehow linked to the way that words are used by the patient to obtain bodily care and contact. In the case of Mr X, his particular use, or rather non-use, of words can be seen when he seeks non-speaking bodily care from others, put himself in the hands of the other person but, as it were, no longer functions as an independent and speaking subject. Such a situation may also be described as 'one-way care.' He wishes for care from the other without any care for the other. By putting himself in the other's hands (including the analyst), he feels he is no longer the subject of his actions and hence has no words of his own. He feels that he has become a non-existent subject and that he is an object to be used. When I say that he does not use words I should say really that words, if used at all, function to obtain a response from the other, i.e., to seduce the other. Quite often this function of words is accompanied by a subtle and seductive use of silence, interspersed with the occasional emotionally charged phrase or bodily movement. In this way, words are not used to reveal but to revel. Thus, when faced with the analytic situation, in which he has to face the daunting possibility of becoming a subject and the owner of his own words, and also has to face the analyst (at some level) as the 'word-giving' father and provider of symbolic context, the patient is both surprised, shocked, and to some extent confused about what to do.

Background

Mr X was in his 30s and had a good and responsible job. He came into analysis with several difficulties in dealing with his fellow employees, and because he experienced recurrent feelings of depression, which were occasionally suicidal in intensity; and, in addition, he had great problems in forming a sustained relationship. As far as he was concerned when he began analysis, he had always been and wished to remain gay. As the analysis subsequently pieced together, his sexual life was exceedingly barren. He had had no last-ing relationship of any sort, and he spent most of his time in casual sexual encounters and one-night stands; hence, I think he was essentially borderline in the way he related.

He spent many evenings in gay clubs and pubs, the sources of his pick-ups. He also occasionally picked up men from toilets or had a sexual encounter in the toilet itself. Even the more satisfactory one-night stands left him feeling depressed and lonely the morning after, when he could hardly bear to look at the man with whom he was sharing the bed. Mr X tended to be more a pas-sive than active sexual partner, although this attitude varied.

Mr X described a close, intimate relationship with his mother, and a distant, unsatisfactory relationship with his father. He partly explained this difference in his relationships with his parents by the fact that his older brother was close to his father, while Mr X was his 'mother's son.' Despite Mr X's description, the mother comes across as distant, puritanical, and emotionally undemonstrative, although a much stronger personality than her husband with, in addition, pre-tensions towards refinement. The father seems to have spent much of his time at work, at the pub, in front of the television, and at football matches with the older brother. Altogether, one obtains a picture of a 'faceless' mother, and a shadowy father. When she was pregnant with the patient the mother suffered from severe toxaemia, and the story went round in the family that she and the patient almost died together. Despite being his mother's son, Mr X was in fact quite neglected. For example, he would spend hours playing alone, especially when he waited for his mother to return from work.

He described one scene which captures the situation: He has returned from primary school, lets himself in the house, and goes up to his room, where he takes out and plays with his little toy theatre. He closes the blinds of the room so that he is in the dark, and then he switches on the theatre lights and makes up a play. But all the while, he is afraid that if the blinds are opened, for example, by his mother, the light will come in and ruin his private show; he will be left with nothing, and it will be the end of the illusion. This memory also captures the feel of the analysis very much. One has the impression of a lonely man whose inner world is fragile and private, and who is afraid that insight and understanding will expose him to something destructive, or at any rate will ruin his private, and at times, near delusional world. Yet there is also the more hopeful and playful side which is fragile and easily deflated.

Mr X remembered being attracted to boys from an early age. From puberty, he would often take part in mutual masturbation with other boys and soon acquired the reputation for leading on the others. His masturbation fantasies have always involved males. As a child, he disliked rough games like football and preferred to play with girls. However, it was only when he was about 24 that he was finally convinced that he was gay. He had several girlfriends in his early 20s; and, as I discovered late in the analysis, he managed full penetra-tion with one girl, whom he had been dating for a year, even though he said it meant nothing to him.

Mr X displayed several symptoms, showing a wide spectrum of disturbance – including depression, separation anxiety, a propensity for acting out, and paranoid anxieties.

These are some of the major (disguised) facts about the history, the most relevant of which to this paper are the stifling mother and the uninvolved father, the shadowy nature of both parents, the impression of Mr X's lonely and emotionally deprived childhood, his apparently fragile inner world, his experiencing of severe and suicidal depressions, and his inability to have intimate relationships.

Account of the Analysis

Some General Features

A general feature of the analysis was that Mr X frequently did not begin to speak immediately or soon after lying on the couch but instead waited in silence, for sometimes as much as 20–30 minutes. At the same time, I was often alert in this silence. I think that this countertransference response may be linked to Mr X's wish to hold my attention in a special and intimate way, which does not involve verbal understanding. (It may also be linked to some unconscious wish on his part to attempt to direct my attention from any source of his anxiety.)

He explained the silence in several ways. His most common explanation was that he is so confused and all over the place before the session that he needed time to collect himself, and to get his fragmented thoughts into some kind of order ready for talking about. We tackled the issue of silence throughout the analysis, and it seems to have several other meanings. One predominant theme is his basic feeling that he really should not be having to speak to me, and that his having got his body to the consulting room and then having managed to lie on the couch should be enough for him to do. Particularly in the early period of the analysis, he could have stayed virtually motion-less and speechless and quite happy, in a state of what he called a 'relaxed trance,' if I had not broken the spell by speaking. Although he was reluctant to speak himself, and at times silences were a manifestation of resistance, he was quite happy for me to speak; indeed, in some ways, he preferred it. The sound of my voice and the number of times I had spoken were as important to him as any meaning. He began to see that there were clear links between this way of listening to me and the way that his mother spoke for him, not encouraging his individuality. Another factor which tended to keep him silent was that he preferred his private thoughts (as he preferred his private childhood theatre game) when he could imagine and fantasize, to talking. He felt that his private ideas were spoiled by speech. In addition, he feared that talking would reveal his vulnerability, or that if he talked, he would be contradicted. Furthermore, several of his introductory silences could be seen as silent sulks, a technique he used when he felt angry with his mother. We subsequently tackled the defensive and aggressive way that he wished to control me by the manner in which he began his sessions. There is also the element of trying to seduce me by soft talking and the creation of a nearly wordless hypnotic state, or reverie; while at the same time, he felt that he was having to control something chaotic and fragmenting, which he expressed in terms of having bits of thoughts confusing his mind which he could not express out loud. Some, but not all, of these thoughts were clearly sexual in content.

Details of the Sessions

I saw Mr X in analysis for a few years. There were many sessions in which little seems to have happened and in which he said little, or what he said was quite controlled. Indeed, the theme of the paper is very much linked with trying to understand this clinical fact.

In the first sessions, Mr X was preoccupied with trying to avoid disagreements with me and was afraid of having what he called a 'difference of opinion.' He also talked about how his parents often disagreed and were different, as they had little in common and rarely had a dialogue. He wanted constant reassurance that we would never disagree and was made very frustrated and anxious by me not doing what he wished. Indeed, the intensity of his anxiety led me to feel that it was touch and go whether Mr X would be able to sustain the analytic relationship, as it represented such a challenge to his previous way of relating.

In the following months, however, some of the details were clarified about how he sought bodily care. What became clear was that he wished for crude body intimacy rather than any emotional intimacy. What he liked most from his casual sexual partners was being held in the other's arms, with little awareness of the other's existence. He also described how, when excited by someone, he felt that he took on the shape of the other person and would mould himself to them, as if he used the other person as a template. He brought these issues into the analysis by expressing the same wishes towards me. But at the same time, he expressed anger and frustration with analysis, because in it, he had to find means other than using his body to communicate with me, and he disliked the fact that there was no physical contact in analysis.

The wish to merge with me also became a major theme, and in Session one, I think that one can see both this element and some of the other elements I have outlined.

Session One: This was a Monday session. Mr X was silent for five minutes; but there was a strong and not very pleasant smell of rather cheap eau de cologne, which quickly permeated the room, invading it in a most uncomfortable way. This smell was a frequent accompaniment at this time, of sessions in which he said that he felt irritable or depressed, and which involved the cover-up of some kind of anal attack. Indeed, he began to talk about his depressed weekend. He said that it had been bad, he had felt lousy, depressed, and full of bad feelings, and added that he was glad to be in the session. He said that he needed people a lot but found it difficult to be with them and make contact, and thus, he always felt lonely. By Saturday, he had felt panicky, whereas in the past he had usually been able to survive until Sunday without too much trouble. He added that he had very much wanted to come to his session this weekend. He had wanted a session, but he said that he didn't know why, because as soon as he's in the session, he feels as if he's been hauled before the teacher, and it's very uncomfortable. I was still aware of the pungent smell, which seemed to be indicative of some wish to invade me, as well as communicating his sense of feeling smelly and full of badness; but I thought that I would acknowledge his sense of loss over the weekend. I said that perhaps he was saying that he had felt in need of me this weekend. There was a weighty pause, and then he said that he didn't like the idea that he needed me at all.

I then said that perhaps he had felt the need to see me over the weekend, but this had then made him feel anxious. This made some sense to him, but he was still very uncomfortable with the idea of needing or missing me. However, after a silence, he then went on to talk about how he dealt with needs in general. He said that they were never met. He added that he had a big ache in his body, which would only be satisfied by the excitement of physical sexual contact. But then he quickly went on to tell me what he was probably most anxious about in his session – his merging with people – his own word. He said that he was aware that sometimes he merges with people and gets right into them. He had done this through body contact. It was exciting but then frightening. I interpreted that perhaps he was afraid that this might happen with me, and that this weekend, he had been aware that he had wished it to happen with me. He agreed, although he also emphasized that he needed body contact for this to happen. I then commented that this wish to merge with people might make it difficult to relate to them and to make emotional contact, something he had complained about at the beginning of the session. He agreed and went on to talk about how he felt he needed to control himself in case he might merge with the other person; he was aware that this way of relating was unsatisfactory in the long run, but he explained that it had the effect of giving him immediate relief for his ache, and he also found it very exciting and so difficult to contemplate giving up in any way.

I interpreted that he was perhaps describing not only a way of comforting himself and of releasing tension (and so giving relief to the ache), but also a way of eliminating feelings of dependency, and I linked this directly with his mixed feelings over wanting and not wanting a session with me over the weekend. This made some limited sense to him. And then he talked about how he is very sensitive to my responses. He said he was aware that this was a session in which he and I had talked more than usual. He worries a lot about the silences, and what is going on in my mind. I commented that if he were worrying so much about what was going on in my mind, it might make it difficult to think about his own mind and to have thoughts. He agreed, and he himself linked this to his childhood when he worried what his mother thought of him. He remembered sitting by the fire and his mother wanting to know what he was doing and thinking. And she would often laugh at him. At other times, he felt that whenever she was angry or preoccupied, she must have been thinking about him. At the same time, he said that there was little warmth from her, and he hardly remembers any body contact with her. I linked the lack of body contact with his mother to his current preoccupations with trying to obtain body contact from his casual partners, which made a little sense to him. This was the end of the session.

I was left feeling somewhat uncomfortable, as if in a way I had been invaded, and yet I also felt that at least we had got somewhere in that he had communicated the hopelessness about his invasiveness. I would speculate that this recurrent use of pungent perfume was indicative of a wish both to cover up his anal attack and to merge body boundaries in order to deny separateness. The wish to merge seemed to be due to the fact that he had been faced by the uncomfortable feeling over the weekend that he might wish to come to analysis and thus might feel dependent on me.

Over the next months, and continuing for some while, Mr X developed a strong maternal transference to me, in which he seemed to want to remain forever undisturbed and constantly cared for by me, forever inside mother, with little individuality of his own. This left me feeling very uncomfortable, and as if I had been forced to take total responsibility for him. The following example, though apparently richer in verbal content than many sessions, is typical of this time.

Session Two: This was a Thursday session. He arrived five minutes late. He then went through an elaborate ritual before lying on the couch, which was a frequent accompaniment of sessions at this time. It consisted of his rather slowly removing his coat, shoes, and contact lenses. After five minutes of silence, he said that he had thought of continuing from the previous day's session, but now felt that he did not want to, as he wished to have a rest, take things easily, and did not want to go too quickly. In the previous session, he had talked a little about how he wished to fit in with his friends and do what they wanted to do, rather than what he had wanted to do. However, I was finding it hard remembering this topic, I did not know what to say in this session, and my thinking processes felt paralyzed. So, I remained silent. After a long silence, he started to talk about how he did not like differences; for example, he did not like differences of opinion. I had felt rather strange in the long silence, as if I could not think, and felt that the session was becoming quite mad. However, after he had spoken I suddenly began to recall the previous session, and I interpreted that perhaps today he had been continuing yesterday's session about disliking differences and wanting to fit in with his friends, by saying at the beginning of the session that he wanted things to stay as they were, with nothing happening, so that there would be no difference in the way that he was, i.e., no change. After a pause, he responded by saying that he felt that people could not understand each other unless they were experiencing the same thing. I commented that it sounded as if he had to make the other person, including me, feel the same as he was, i.e., with no change. After a pause, he responded by saying that he felt that people could not understand each other unless they were experiencing the same thing. I commented that it sounded as if he had to make the other person, including me, feel the same as he did.

After a somewhat anxious pause, he began to talk about how this kind of thing happened when he had sex. He explained that what he obtained from sex was close and intense physical contact, which he could not get elsewhere. But he said that he had difficulty getting close emotionally. He explained that he wished to be cuddled and looked after. He added that he could do without the sex if he got the close emotional experience. I commented that it seemed as if he was looking to be mothered, and that sex was the nearest he was saying he could to it. He agreed and then talked about being scared of involving himself with people in case they were frightened by him, and by how much he needed to be mothered. He then talked about his mother. In fact, unusually he had phoned her the previous day. He said that the usual thing had happened, i.e., he did not have to think as she spoke for him and filled in all the silences. He added that it had always been the same, so he did not have to be independent. He said that because of this it was difficult for him now to talk. He preferred to listen to others and fit in with them. I interpreted that perhaps telephoning his mother had had quite an impact on him, and that at the beginning of the session, he had wanted me to be like her, and to leave him in peace, or else fill in all the silences; and that he had wanted me to fit in with this wish. He agreed with this and then made an interesting slip of the tongue. He said that he had always wanted to be like 'My husband... I mean my mother.' He laughed a little and, after a pause, explained that he had wanted to be like her; she was better than his father, she was livelier and more interesting, and he liked to fit in with her. I said that perhaps he wanted to fit in with me in some way. He commented that he often waited for me to say something. This excited him a lot, and he liked to hear my voice. But what he found difficult was when I did not understand him or when I had a different viewpoint. I interpreted that perhaps I might be experienced by him as someone like a father, rather than a mother who would do all the talking for him. This made some sense to him, and it was the end of the session.

I felt that this was a complicated session, and that there were several themes only, some of which I could begin to grasp. I certainly felt that Mr X had to make the other person feel the same, and this process, perhaps one of projective identification, was active at the beginning of the session, when I felt paralyzed and unable to use words. It may have been that this was not only a way of keeping me at bay defensively, and of stopping change, but also of communicating in a concrete way his confusion – for example, the confusion which would follow from a denial of difference between, say, mother and husband, as revealed later in the session by the slip of the tongue. In many of the sessions, it was exceedingly difficult overcoming the paralysis of talking, and I was often left feeling helpless and occasionally angry. I think that the ritual with the clothes at the beginning of the session may have been linked with a wish for me merely to look at what he was doing rather than talk and face him with his conflicts.

Subsequent sessions involved something of a shift in that Mr X began to find his silences to be difficult, irritating, and painful, rather than only me. He had felt that analysis made him silent, but now he became more aware that analysis revealed, and hopefully dealt with, his wish not to communicate verbally. However, there have really been only minimal changes in the way he used his analysis. There were only glimpses of a positive paternal transference, and some hints of a clearer negative transference. There were many times when he did not want me to irritate him with what was going on in his inner world, and yet other times when he wanted me to penetrate his inner world in a very intimate way and without speaking. Indeed, one may often wonder if he had any therapeutic alliance at all, yet the fact that he continued to attend his analysis for some years may be indicative of some wish for insight.

Third session: Although most sessions involved my having to tolerate long silences and considerable denial of anxiety, this session does show some attempt on Mr X's part to get to grips with his emotional life.

It was a Wednesday session, and he came seven minutes late. He said with some annoyance that he had left at the usual time, but the traffic had been exceptionally bad. He added that he was particularly annoyed as he had wanted to come on time. His being late reminded him of, to use his own word, his ambivalence about coming, which made him feel uncomfortable. After a pause, he added that he was also thinking that from today his fees were to go up, and he was probably annoyed about that too, and that he had wasted valuable money by being late. I pointed out that by being late he had used the time at the old rate of fees, in terms of money per minute. He laughed at this comment and said that he could see this. Then he added that he had often thought that I only wanted his money. I commented that his attitude made it difficult to know what he wanted from me. He replied that he did not know what he wanted. He had originally wanted someone to talk to who would help him with his problems and confusions. He had not realized how difficult it was going to be, and all the trouble he had to go through. I interpreted that it sounded as if a main trouble was having to face his wish not to be here, and his annoyance with me for charging him for my listening. He agreed but then said how much better his work was since being in analysis, and how often he used what we had discussed to help him deal with his working relationships. I acknowledged what he said but added that it sounded as if he were avoiding the issue of his angry feelings about me. He said with some difficulty that this was something he intensely disliked. What he would like, he continued, was to come to the session, just pay me, and nothing more would happen, that there would be no change and nothing said. I pointed out that there had been a change in the fee, which had obviously annoyed him and perhaps helped him to be late to the session.

He granted that this may have been true, to some extent. I continued by saying that perhaps he was also saying that he would like not to need me at all, and that the increase in fee had perhaps reminded him of the commitment that analysis represented. And I made a link with his relationship to his mother, in that perhaps he was expressing a wish to pay off his mother in some way, provide her with the supplies (or money, in this instance), but did not want to use her. He agreed and said that he felt as if it must be doing him good if he's paying all this money, rather like the Christian idea of giving away all one's gold. But, he added, he did not then like to do any work. I clarified that it seemed to me that the work he did not wish to do was that of facing conflict, like facing why he did not want to come to the session, despite the good that the sessions could also do. There was a long silence, in which he seemed to be taking in the interpretation.

He then went on to talk about the coming weekend, in which he said there would be a 'programme of conflicts' that he did not like, having to face pressure from his friends to go out with them. He then told a story about a man who had come round the previous night and whom he had waved to in a car the previous weekend. This man had clearly desired Mr X and had turned up at his house. His immediate response was to say to him, 'What are you doing here? Has your television broken down?' He realized in the session that he had been aggressive to this man and added that at the time he had felt that the man had merely wished to exploit him by, for example, using his colour television. I commented that perhaps he had been afraid of something. He replied that he had been afraid of being friendly, in case he had been overwhelmed by friendliness in a gushing way. I finally interpreted, with some agreement from him, that perhaps his fear was that he would be overwhelmed by a wish to exploit me aggressively and just pay for his session without speaking about himself and his conflicts.

Discussion

I have tried to indicate in the clinical material how difficult it may be for a borderline patient to take the step from being in the middle of a primitive transference to being aware through words of their primitive relationship to the analyst, and how this may put strain on the analyst's capacity to think and remain unconfused. An indication of some therapeutic success is perhaps Mr X's slight ability in the last example to make verbal sense of his attacks on me, and his revealing some awareness of the perverse areas of the transference, e.g., his wish to exploit me and treat me as if all I wanted were money, and perhaps too his awareness that words for him are a debased currency.

Although there were only small changes in the day-to-day work of the analysis, it is true to say that Mr X stopped trying to pick up men in toilets, he enlarged his interests, received promotion at work, and began to attempt some more intimate relationships.

One could say that enactment of primitive fantasies involves a complicated and obsessive 'script,' or 'scenario,' in which the body, imagination, and the eye, and to a greater or lesser extent, the word, are all urgently involved. One could describe some primitive scripts as made for talkies, while others, as in Mr X's case, are made for silent films. As Stoller[3] has pointed out, in such scripts there seems to be present a basic trauma, over which the patient is attempting to triumph. In Mr X's case, this trauma may have been a mother-child relationship devoid of much physical contact and emotionality; and in addition, a father who paid more attention to Mr X's older brother than to himself. One might conjecture that the memory of playing with the toy theatre is also central in understanding the primitive script and the nature of the hypothesized trauma. In his solitary play, he seemed to be trying to create the illusion of care and concern in order to deal with what he experienced as, and probably was, real neglect. At the same time, in his maternal transference to me, he seemed to be reliving both a desperate wish for wordless and primary bodily dependency on the mother and an aggressive denial of the role of the father.

There may be some truth in the somewhat simplistic idea that one of my main analytic functions was to promote thinking and to help enable Mr X to use his linguistic capacities. In this sense, one might suggest that one of my main functions as an analyst was to lend him my thinking and to provide him with an auxiliary interpretive agency until he could provide his own. Analytic understanding could then be seen, in this context, as the provision of a notation for the patient whose inner world is very confused or dominated by sensations and crude bodily states. The analyst as the provider of symbolic context can help such patients by introducing a principle of order and regularity, and an important part of the therapeutic alliance is the patient's experience of the analyst as a person interested in giving meaning, with, however, great respect for the patient's mind. Indeed, perhaps one can say that a main use of language is to free thought from the dominance of bodily sensations and crude feelings. As well as finding a language for such states, one is replacing, in analysis, crude sensations by language, or else transforming the crude sensations by means of language into more manageable feelings.

Notes

1   Glasser (1979, p. 163ff).
2   Freud (1911, p. 17).
3   Stoller (1976).

11 Outtakes

Extracts from Journal 1976 to 2025

Language games are vital in order to structure one's experience and to free thought from the dominance of sensations. But there is a price to be paid – alienation from nature, and suffering.

> The problem of the unsayable, the negative object, the unsayable impossible object.
> The problem of illumination, uncreated light (Duns Scotus)
> The mother's point of light.
> Curiosity and the appetite of the eye.

Augustine – The individual on the mountain who sees the pure light above and the mist below.

The fading of the subject – may have something to do with waking up and forgetting the dream or going to sleep. Or to something about the whole structure of what we call the subject, an unstable structure that constantly fades, whose light goes out, that dies. Or to the fact that when you have reached some point you can understand, what you think is truth, then clearly it is not the whole story. You erase and recreate, and so it goes on.

Certain artists like Giotto, Cézanne, Rembrandt, draw us into their pictures, so that we almost touch the objects depicted, or they almost look at us. But when we try to discuss what happens, something is lost or missing. As there is always something unknowable about us, which they touch.

Thoughts about Cézanne. He had quite a lot to say about the artistic process, often emphasizing the need for the artist to restrain ordinary perception and control and allow another more receptive process to take place. This other process is presumably somewhere in touch with the unconscious. I say somewhere because I'm not sure quite where the boundary between consciousness and unconscious would be. It is very ambiguous. The strange nature of oil paint is a medium itself, as Francis Bacon has emphasized, makes it uncertain how is conscious and how much unconscious while the artist is at work. And after all, the work itself, the application of paint on the canvas or paper, has its own momentum. So, one brushstroke leads to another one, work brings up hew horizons and new problems. Maybe with Cézanne

DOI: 10.4324/9781003683315-11

the issue for him was that he had a powerful vision of what he was aiming towards, but a terrible struggle with the actual brushstrokes. Perhaps the work is so emotionally engaging because of this very struggle. One may make a comparison with Beethoven's creative struggles. As well as the process of letting be, Cézanne also describes a synthesizing role of the artist's 'temperament,' which brings together the various fragments of sensations and enables the artist to realize his vision or his 'motif.' Certainly, Cézanne believed that the artist had to paint with feeling, otherwise the work would be dead, an academic exercise. Cézanne was so revolutionary as he presents us with a new vision of the world, overturning traditional means of representation. Instead of the old Cartesian, a view of the human subject looking out at a world with a mini little world inside him which reflected the outside world, he shows a different way of seeing. Which of course, became the basis for much of modern art. Cézanne presents us with the issue of subjectivity itself, or temperament as he called it. He represented the encounter between him and the object. There had been precedents in the romantic movement, and Cézanne was impressed by Delacroix. But he was also more classical and engaged with more than just an emotional response, but with formal relationships.

Why does the hallucinating subject obey a voice? For example, if the voice says you must go and kill yourself. The voice is not simply a perception, an object perceived outside like ordinary voices with which one can have a rational conversation, or which one can reject or agree with. A hallucinated voice is a *percepiens*. It is of the subject and when it says go and kill yourself, it is really the subject saying go and kill yourself. And thus, he obeys himself, only he rejects the notion consciously.

What does psychosis mean for the psychiatric patient? An illness. A particular reaction. A message indicated something is not well in the family or themselves. Feeling of precarious subjectivity.

Tustin – The heartbreak at the centre of human existence – separation, the realization of body separateness and the relation of the individual to others question. The autistic object not differentiated from body stuff. The capsulation in autism; the modification of relations with the other; less reading of cues, more rigidity, less give and take and flow, brittleness.

Tustin describes how the therapist, by a process of imaginative reconstruction of primitive experience, lends the patient his thinking and provides an auxiliary interpretative agency until he can provide his own. I would add that, especially with such children, the therapist's mind helps to introduce a principle of order and regularity, that an important part of the therapeutic alliance is his experience of the therapist as a person interested in giving meaning, in trying to cut out shapes with his help out of his confused, indistinct mass of sensations and signs – with, however, great respect for the patient's mind, Indeed, perhaps one can say that a main use of language is to free thought from the dominance of sensations And that as well as finding a language for sensations, one is replacing crude sensations by language; or else transforming the crude sensations, by means language, into more manageable feelings.

Groups – forces keeping them together and forces keeping them apart

The writer, especially the poet, has the realm of the undefined, the unsaid, constantly before them. It retreats as they approach a word, when they touch language's source.

The neurotic lives in the law, suffers and wants to be well within the law. The schizophrenic suffers from something else. Compare the latter with Kafka's Trial where the law is outside, never stated. K is possessed by it. But there is no effective law only the symbol of the law. He meets the symbolic law, for example, in the court. Law in Kafka is ever present but indefinite, like a paranoid delusion.

Functions of language – small talk, socializing, and various other functions. In schizophrenia – hiding type language, joke language, schizophrenic small talk, poetic language, word salad.

Compare psychosis to a dream backwards. On waking from a dream, you feel that there were connections between events, but that all seemed absurd. In psychosis, there is a similar situation but in reverse. Everything suddenly acquires connections which were unthought or undreamt of. In that sense, it is akin to a creative act.

Different kinds of spontaneity. Spontaneity of the unconscious captured in jokes irruption into consciousness. The unexpected. The realm of surprise. Spontaneity of response in thought and feeling. The latter possible for the analyst in occasionally. Spontaneity in personal encounters. Freedom and spontaneity. Freedom to relate. Political spontaneity – uprising, Trotsky, Havel.

Split transference. Certain patients, e.g., after a psychotic breakdown, as the father transference is approached then quickly fear about being taken over by the mother, or vice versa. Or a flight from the transference. Linked to early failure to integrate the two primary objects.

The analyst's interest in the past is really for the purpose of explaining the present. Which is much less true of most historians. Psychoanalysts interpret the developing process, aiming at psychic experience rather actual events. Although it may be important to have some sense of the reality of an experience. The day-to-day work of the analyst a bit like the meticulous work of the historian in the archive. The two-fold function of history – the historian/psychoanalyst helps sort out the patient's material but also helps to break up unities and deconstructs and decentres the listening experience, creating new meaning. The past is transformed into a history.

Freud in Civilization and its discontents. The image of archaeological memory, with all the sights intact. The psychical object is preserved in a strange sort of archaeological field made up of fixed and shifting elements. Engulfment of Pompeii and burial of Tutankhamun compared to repression as cataclysm and burial in the unconscious.

The signs that are waiting for someone who can respond to the elusiveness of the patient's subjectivity and try to help them speak authentically. Restoring to life. Compare to a musical score bringing the music to life.

Psychotic depression. The other is not there when missed. There is nothing there to be missed. The depression covers and covers over, comes in place of what is missing.

Hegel – Nature goes in cycles, history goes in spirals; it never repeats itself. Apparent repetitions are always differentiated by acquiring something new. Compare to psychoanalytic repetition.

Historical imagination (Collingwood). History is a combination of a perception of the here and now and of abstract thought that apprehends the everywhere and always, the transient and the reasoned knowledge of abstract entities. The historian is constantly selecting, constructing and criticizing. Imagination is the activity which bridges the gaps between what authorities tell us and gives the historical narrative or description its continuity. The historian's picture of his subject appears as a web of imaginative construction stretched between certain fixed points provided by the statements of their authorities. Compare with the authority of the patient. The web of imaginative construction as the touchstone to establish alleged facts as genuine or not. Use in the analytic setting. The past can only be understood from a perspective. The past is not dead but living on in the present. The past as reenactable between people the psychoanalytic principle – Collingwood modified.

The past in psychoanalysis may come up as what has not been understood or felt or transformed. Obviously, trauma being the obvious example. So, there is the past that is available for memory. Then there is the past that may be just enacted. For example, a patient not turning up for some sessions regularly. That could be bringing something from the past that has not been metabolized. The absences may be evidence of something that needs to be understood, not just acting out.

How are we able to know the mind of another? This raises many fundamental questions about the nature of our minds and about what psychoanalysts are up to when they treat people. In a sense, a psychoanalyst takes it for granted that the other person is knowable to some extent at least. There would not be much point in seeing someone for analysis if one thought that the other was a complete puzzle. It may take a long time in analysis to begin to make sense of what the other person is about. It can take time to become familiar with the other's way of being, to appreciate their own subjective view of the world; though there are times when issues are reasonably clear from the beginning, at least in a general way. On the other hand, there is much we do not know about the other person, and perhaps can never know; as well as areas that are untouched, or are only barely known.

What Husserl called the paradox of human subjectivity – the fact that the human being is both a subject for the world and at the same time an object in the world. There seem to be many ways of what we mean by an objective as opposed to a subjective understanding of humans. There seem to be at least three ways of seeing this problem. First, to attempt to eliminate the distinction as Husserl and Dewey attempted. Second, to focus more on the subjective understanding as, for example, Kierkegaard and Sartre, proposed. And thirdly to attempt to find a place for both the subjective and the objective realms as Thomas Nagel has suggested.

Faith is the realm of personal meaning, ethics the realm of commitment.
Spectrum of being in the world/alienation from one's own being.
The game as the prototypical subjective organization.

The many voices of consciousness. Yet the many voices still have the quality of consciousness, fleeting here and gone. Consciousness not a single defile. Consciousness is a multiple type of structure adapted to man social being. Taking account of multiple realities, many voices, many subjects. Compare to a fugue made up of independent voices which yet makes a new reality. In psychoanalysis, we hear voices emerging out of the unconscious.

Losing oneself in a novel is pleasurable not for the escape as such, but because entering the story is to enter into a deep relation to our subjectivity.

Home as a place to just sleep. Or as a place to live.

Therapy – helping to find a sense of belonging and location, dwelling in the world rather than retreating from it.

We must go beyond the subject/object relationship. But we cannot really do that yet. We still have the old tools that have to be used. But something else is constantly pushing to break away. Which is clear in Freud. Merleau-Ponty cites the visible as the common stuff. Heidegger talks about being.

Merging and petrification as two ways of stultifying otherness and closing off the subjective world.

Of course there are self-experiences from within. But it is in answering the other, in encounters and the meeting of two consciousness that produces the whole human response. The social response.

Undoing the negative, a constant task psychoanalytic treatment.

Rites of passage. Symbolic acts which unite the individual with a group or ways of bringing the individual into relation with the group. Having a place, becoming a subject. Marking the passage into full subjectivity.

My notion of subjective organization is really more a way of thinking. Starting to define an area of study, an area of experience. So, I can begin to map out field, to start making new contributions. It means revising old theories, but of course there are doubts and certainties and inherent difficulties in the model. This doesn't mean stop seeing how the model may help, even if in the end we must discard it.

Creating a place to survive is one of the earliest basics of the subject's structure.

Looking at the legal system in different ways. First, an ideal model, the concept, the notion of a ground rule, etc. Next, the reality in the day-to-day of what happens. Thirdly, historical elements, some of which are repressed. And lastly, the unconscious deep structures embedded in the legal system, about which people may or may not be consciously aware, e.g., some assumptions about human behaviour, how groups are formed.

Creating a lived experience in psychoanalysis not just imparting understanding.

Problem of subjectivity. It is inevitable that we come up against some basic philosophical and sociological problems in psychoanalysis. For example, is the subject is given or constructed? Socially constructed or what? If the subject is socially constructed, we need to examine this process. If society is built up by activity that expresses subjective meaning, what we mean by subjectivity here. Can we use psychoanalytic experience to flesh out the question and reframe our notions of subjectivity? We need to look at the notion of social structure and its place and function in the structure of the subject. As the subject is a notion that embraces the individual and social fields. It has a dual structure. An example of how individuals can bolster up the social world. Havel's Power of the Powerless. When everyone stops believing in a system and it no longer functions. So there needs to be a fundamental sceptical attitude to the system. The system needs to be open to debate and change or else subjects are frozen.

Face-to-face sessions can be interactive but also can encourage evasions. The couch with its elimination of the face-to-face encounter, an *epoché* of sorts, reveals subjectivity in all its power and fleetingness.

Nietzsche – the invention of the subject.

The horror of loneliness given the constitutional sociability of mankind.

Differentiate the analyst reacting to the patient as in one form of counter-transference from the analyst's subjective response as part of intersubjective communication.

Disruptions to subjectivity as in abuse cases.

Enid Balint and unconscious communication – e.g., the patient having to experience the subjective reality of, say the grandparent, communicated via the parent. That is, a piece of split-off, dissociated element of subjective experience. A piece of the mother's subjectivity which has remained unconscious and not allowed to be experienced as subjective, cut off from its moorings and context. Experience 'by proxy.'

Practice, being embedded in human life, often runs ahead of theory.

Irony in psychoanalysis. Socrates both disavows he has knowledge yet clearly does have wisdom. Cf the analyst who both disclaims knowing the 'truth' yet also answers through interpretations etc., with a skill in reading the unconscious.

Analyst's presence and absence. Being with, being there, being behind, and letting-be.

The oedipal constellation is in the end about taking up a position, one way or another with respect to desire. E.g., the male or female position etc. At the cost of the other position. However, clinical experience reveals how difficult taking up a position can be for some people, how people may hover between positions, or be confused and cannot assume their desire. In classical Oedipus complex there is the fantasy of the rival's death or elimination, such as the killing of the father; one element must be pushed aside in order to take up one's own position. The 'third position' stabilizes shifting identifications. The hysterical identification in Freud as a special kind of unstable identification.

Recounting past events in the session creates history.

Different kinds of 'between.' Between solid parents etc. Between many people with the attachment, for example, floating in space looking for a gravitational pull.

History as multiple representations of the past. In the transference, the historical element includes the past and the present and reworking of the past.

With the patient – the rhythm of the history of the events. But also, another kind of historical rhythm, the unconscious and timelessness.

Differentiate the analyst as witness and as reconstructive historian.

One danger of historical retrospective reconstruction is the sense of fatality that the past is set and there is no contingency. So, one needs to allow for surprise and uncertainty, limiting fatalism. The same goes with psychoanalytic explanations.

The debris of psychotic breakdown.

Oakeshott – Differentiates practical past from the historical past. And psychoanalysis. We deal with both. Or in parallel. We hear the practical past, but we cover in the process of analysis the historical past. Or we convert the practical to historical past. Psychoanalytical history as the story of the subject's traces, fossil footprints. The past is carried in various ways by the subject, in relationship, recollection, in the stream of lived experience. Transference *from* the past, repeating the past in therapy or in relationships. Transference *to* the past, distorting ones view of the past from the present.

Shakespeare's dramatic spaces – green spaces, islands, new arrivals, sometimes tolerant spaces, dream-space, wild heath where Lear is turned out of his homes, places outside the court; often confusion, or storm, and then resolution of conflicts, rebalancing of distorted loves. Identities are alter-ed. Although there is often no simple resolution. C.f. having a therapeutic space outside the home in order to reconcile opposites and tolerate differences and refind a sense of home.

Shakespeare challenges comfortable notions of identity and difference, strangeness and familiarity, challenges the 'thinking as usual' approach of comfortable home life, the boundary between the known and the unknown, what is beneath surface appearances. Pervading many of the dramas – the question of where one's true home is.

Intolerance as destroying society's social relations. Makes it impossible for different communities to communicate, home is no longer a safe place. No harm principle and respect principle needed together to counter intolerance.

Tolerance a stage before acceptance. Negative tolerance, putting up with, positive tolerance as a virtue. Building bridges not walls. 'Live and let live,' i.e., accept different ways of life.

Tolerance in psychoanalysis – of the other, of the other in oneself (the internalized other), of the unconscious.

Organ tolerance after transplant – needing medication to accept a foreign graft. Or engineering tolerance – having enough capacity in a system to ensure it will operate even when some parts fail. But not drug tolerance of addicts.

Tolerance of the unconscious, some patients find difficult, yet necessary to function effectively.

Different kinds of spaces – private space (home); sacred space (church, temple etc.); public space (park, street); institutional space (school, hospital, etc.). Each space regulated differently, e.g., private space as free from intrusion, institutional the most regulated. Psychoanalytic protected setting a conjunction of private, sacred and institutional areas.

Moving musical performances – e.g., attending Allegri quartet. There is a human context, intense communication between the players, intense in the way that poetry is complex and condensed, intensifying the experience. Music can move us because it expresses sadness etc. not by making us sad, though it can also do that. Moved by the sadness in a Shostakovich quartet but also uplifted, transformed.

The aesthetic emotion as part of our emotional equipment going back to the joy of creating something as a child, matching the flow and contours of the inner life, the inner music.

The many ways of listening to music – the sheer beauty of the musical patterns, the wonder at the complexity of themes brought into a unity (Bach), the expression of complex emotional states including awe and inner contemplation, bringing into renewed focus the flow of our inner life, if narrative such as lieder or opera or musicals there can be the interest in plots and characters bringing into relief deep truths about human relationships through the logic of the music, incitement to action such as in war, bringing communities together, inducing the desire to dance, consolation of loss, wistful nostalgia (Elgar), triumphant acceptance of human endeavour (Nielsen), icy tragic loneliness (Sibelius's Tapiola). Communication involves emotion, so music obviously then incorporates some emotion however 'pure.' Taking us on a musical journey.

Think of Puccini's Tosca. There is the beauty of the melodies, but also the tight structure of the music's organization. Recall the way that the church bells come into play at a dramatic point, with the Scarpia theme, the irony of evil against the background of the church bells (c.f. The Godfather christening scene).

The 'full' musical response includes the visual. C.f. Christian Blackshaw piano recital at The Snape. There is a human encounter, the visual quality of his playing as well as the sheer beauty and technical mastery, the lights dimmed, stillness, the spiritual quality of the man coming through, reverence for the music, music's soul.

Essence of evil, cancelling of the human subject. For example, in the film Shoah the way the guards dealt with the digging up of corpses and their burning. They were not to be called corpses or victims, but figures or *Schatten*, shit.

The radioactive nature of evil. Evil tries to limit the other as subject; kill, hurt, freeze, confine, torture etc. all ways of eliminating the other as subject. Evil as the absence of presence. What about malign presence? Lesser evils lead to greater evils.

Different kinds of perpetrators of evil an industrial scale. Individual perpetrators, experts like doctors and lawyers, desk perpetrators, grassroots killers, uniformed perpetrators. It's a denial of subjectivity and the killer themselves as well as the victim. Both elements are needed in order to kill people in this way.

Hateful ideologies are often around underground, waiting to be released again when societies' conditions are favourable to them. Should we pay more attention to the signs? Look at different ways that the individual's drives are modified, controlled, sublimated, diverted for the sake of civilization and civic peace. Or on the contrary, how these drives can be whipped up by populists and their manifestation intensified, at times of war, for example, and economic depression.

Psychotic implants or injections or grafts infecting groups of ordinary people. Releasing them from ordinary social inhibitions. Civilization is always in the balance, a fine balance; psychotic forces can easily take over the group making it impossible to have sane thoughts.

Even if Mahler felt alienated from the world, he carried his psychic home with him – the pluralistic world of his childhood and adolescence, the mixture of German music, military, nature, church, Jewish, and Bohemian music, incorporated into his symphonies. Music his true psychic home.

Look for the subject's dilemma in their dream associations. The multiple positions or places from where the dream thoughts arise in the unconscious – different from fragmentation. The plurality of voices is not chaotic fragmentation. Amalgamation of the different voices into an idiom or what Cézanne called temperament.

Poets use the dream thoughts to create a poetic dream. Analysts help the patient to find the dream thoughts from the dream.

Bibliography

Anzieu, D. (1995). *The Skin-Ego*, trans. by N. Segal. London: Karnac, 2016.

Arendt, H. (1970). *Men in Dark Times*. New York and London: Harcourt.

Auster, P. (1982). *The Invention of Solitude*. New York: Sun Publishing.

Balint, M. (1948). On the psychoanalytic training system. *Int. J Psychoanal.* 29: 163–173.

Balint, M. (1968). *The Basic Fault*. London: Tavistock.

Barenboim, D. and Said, E. (2002). *Parallels and Paradoxes*. London: Bloomsbury.

Benjamin, J. (1988). *The Bonds of Love: Psychoanalysis, Feminism, and the Bonds of Domination*. New York: Pantheon.

Benjamin, J. (1998). *Shadow of the Other: Intersubjectivity and Gender in Psychoanalysis*. New York and London: Routledge.

Bentovim, A., Elton, A., Hildebrand, J. et al. (1988). *Child Sexual Abuse within the Family: Assessment and Treatment*. London: Butterworth.

Benvenuto, B. and Kennedy, R. (1986). *The Works of Jacques Lacan*. London: Free Association.

Berger, P. and Luckmann, T. (1966). *The Social Construction of Reality*. London: Allen Lane.

Bettleheim, B. (1976). *The Uses of Enchantment*. New York: Alfred Kopf.

Bianchetti, C. (2017). *Il Soggetto Sfuggente*. Bea Bassin: Edizioni Accademiche Italiane.

Bion, W. (1970). *Attention and Interpretation*. London: Tavistock.

Blanchot, M. (1955). *The Space of Literature*, trans. by A. Smock, Lincoln: University of Nebraska Press, 1982.

Bloom, H. (1997). *The Anxiety of Influence*. New York and Oxford: OUP.

Bollas, C. (1989). *Forces of Destiny*. London: Free Association.

Bonheoffer, D. (1970). *Letters and Papers from Prison*, ed. E. Bethege. New York: Touchstone.

Britton, R. (1996). Subjectivity, objectivity and the fear of chaos. *Bulln. Brit. Psychoanal. Soc.* 32: 11–21.

Bromberg, P. (1993). Shadow and substance: A relational perspective on clinical process. *Psychoanal. Psychol.* 10(2): 147–168.

Buber, M. (1970). *I and Thou*, trans. W. Kaufmann. Edinburgh: T. and T. Clark.

Buechler, S. (1998). The analyst's experience of loneliness. *Cont. Psychoanal.* 34: 91–113.

Cavell, M. (1991). The subject of mind. *Int. J. Psycho-Anal.* 72: 141–154.

Celenza, A. and Gabbard, G. O. (2003). Analysts who commit sexual boundary viola-tions. *J. Amer. Psychoanal. Assn.* 51: 617–636.

Chasseguet-Smirgel, J. (1985). *Creativity and Perversion*. London: Free Association Books.

Danon-Boileau, L. (2016). Parole associative, parole compulsive, in *Des Psychanalys-tes en Séance*, ed. L. Danon-Boileau and J-Y. Tamet, pp. 28–29. Paris: Gallimard.

De Nora, T. (2000). *Music in Everyday Life*. Cambridge: Cambridge University Press.

Dewey, J. (1929). *Experience and Nature*. La Salle, IL: Open Court.

Dilthey, W. (1989). *Introduction to the Human Sciences*, ed. R. Makkreel and F. Rodi. Princeton, NJ: Princeton University Press.

Dolto, F. (1994). *Solitude*. Paris: Gallimard.

Ehrlich, H. S. (2003). Working on the frontier and the use of the analyst. *Int. J. Psychoa-nal.* 84(2): 235–247.

Eitingon, M. (1923). Report of the Berlin psycho-analytical policlinic. *Bull. Int. Psy-choanal. Asscn.* 4: 254–269.

Eitingon, M. (1925). Reports of the branch societies. *Bul. Int. Psychoanal. Assn.* 6: 235–23.

Faimberg, H. (2005). *The Telescoping of Generations*. London and New York: Routledge.

Ferenczi, S. (1928). The elasticity of psychoanalytic technique, in *Selected Writings*, ed. Sandor Ferenzci, pp. 255–268. Harmondsworth: Penguin Books, 1999.

Ferenczi, S. (1933). The confusion of tongues between adults and the child, in *Selected Writings*, ed. Sandor Ferenzci, pp. 293–303. Harmondsworth: Penguin Books, 1999.

Fonagy, P. and Target, M. (1996). Playing with reality: I. theory of mind and the normal development of psychic reality. *Int. J. Psycho-Anal.* 77: 217–233.

Freud, S. (1896). The aetiology of hysteria. *The Standard Edition of the Complete Psy-chological Works of Sigmund Freud*. S.E. 3: 191–221.

Freud, S. (1900). *The Interpretation of Dreams*. S.E. 4 and 5. London: Hogarth.

Freud, S. (1909). Family romances. S.E. 9: 235–242.

Freud, S. (1911). The handling of dream interpretation. S.E. 12: 90–96.

Freud, S. (1912). The dynamics of the transference. S.E. 12: 97–108.

Freud, S. (1918). From the history of an infantile neurosis. S.E. 17: 1–124.

Freud, S. (1920). Beyond the pleasure principle. S.E. 18: 1–64.

Freud, S. (1923). The ego and the id. S.E. 19: 1–66.

Freud, S. (1930). Preface to ten years of the Berlin psycho-analytic institute. S.E. 21: 257.

Freud, S. (1937). Analysis terminable and interminable. S.E. 23: 211–253.

Fromm-Reichmann, F. (1990). Loneliness. *Cont. Psychoanal.* 26: 305–329.

Glasser, M. (1979). From the analysis of a transvestite. *Int. Rev. Psycho-Anal.* 6: 163–173.

Godelier, M. (2004). *The Metamorphosis of Kinship*, trans. N. Kelly (2011). London and New York: Verso.

Gratier, M. and Trevarthen, C. (2007). Voice, vitality and meaning. *Int. J. Dialog. Sci.* 2(1): 169–181.

Green, A. (1983). The dead mother, in *On Private Madness* (1986), pp. 142–173. Lon-don: Hogarth Press and Institute of Psychoanalysis.

Green, A. (2003). *Diachrony in Psychoanalysis*. London and New York: Free Associa-tion Books.

Heidegger, M. (1962). *Being and Time*, trans. J. Macquarrie and E. Robinson. Oxford: Blackwell.

Hoffman, I. Z. (1991). Discussion: Toward a social-constructivist view of the psycho-analytic situation. *Psychoanal. Dial.* 1: 74–105.

Hume, D. (1740). *A Treatise of Human Nature*, ed. L. Selby-Bigge. Oxford: Clarendon, 1888.

Husserl, E. (1954). *The Crisis of European Sciences*, trans. D. Carr. Evanston, IL: Northwestern University Press, 1970.

Jones, E. (1961). *The Life and Work of Sigmund Freud*. New York: Basic Books.

Joseph, B. (1982). Addiction to near death. *Int. J. Psychoanal.* 63: 449–456.

Joseph, B. (1989). *Psychic Equilibrium and Psychic Change: Selected Papers of Betty Joseph*, ed. M. Feldman and E. Bott Spillius. London: Routledge.

Kant, I. (1934). *The Critique of Pure Reason*, trans. J. Meikeljohn. London: Everyman.

Kennedy, R. (1984). A dual aspect of the transference. *Int. J. Psycho-Anal.* 65: 471–483.

Kennedy, R. (1990). A severe form of communication disorder in the psychoanalysis of an ill adolescent. *Int. J. Psychoanal.* 71: 309–119.

Kennedy, R. (1996a). Aspects of consciousness - one voice or many? *Psychoanal. Dial.* 6(1): 73–96.

Kennedy, R. (1996b). Bearing the unbearable: Working with the abused mind. *Int. J. Psychoanal. Psychother.* 10(2): 143–154.

Kennedy, R. (1997). On subjective organizations (1997). *Psychoanal. Dial.* 7(S): 553–581.

Kennedy, R. (1998). *The Elusive Human Subject: A Psychoanalytical Theory of Subject Relations*. London: Free Association.

Kennedy, R. (2000). Becoming a subject. *Int. J. Psychoanal.* 81: 875–892.

Kennedy, R. (2002). *The Now of the Past. History, Subjectivity and Psychoanalysis*. London and New York: Brunner-Routledge.

Kennedy, R. (2007). *The Many Voices of Psychoanalysis*. London and New York: Routledge.

Kennedy, R. (2014). *The Psychic Home*. London and New York: Routledge.

Kennedy, R. (2019). *Tolerating Strangers in Intolerant Times*. London and New York: Routledge.

Kennedy, R. (2022). *The Power of Music*. London: Phoenix.

Kennedy, R. (2023). *The Evil Imagination*. London: Phoenix.

Kierkegaard, S. (1941). *Concluding Unscientific Postscript*, trans. D. Swenson and W. Lowrie. Princeton, NJ: Princeton University Press.

King, P. (1978). Affective response of the analyst to the patient's communications. *Int. J. Psychoanal.* 59: 329–334.

Kirschner, S. and Tomasello, M. (2010). Joint music making promote prosocial behaviour in 4-year-old children. *Evol. Hum. Behav.* 31(5): 354–364.

Klauber, J. (1976). Elements of the psychoanalytical relationship, in *Difficulties in the Analytic Encounter*, (1981), pp. 45–62. New York and London: Jason Aronson.

Klein, M. (1963). On the sense of loneliness, in *Envy and Gratitude and Other Works*, ed. Roger Money-Kyrle, pp. 300–313. London: Hogarth Press and Institute of Psychoanalysis.

Kohon, G. (1984). Reflections on dora: The case of hysteria. *Int. J. Psycho-Anal.* 65: 73–84.

Kojève, A. (1980). *Introduction to the Reading of Hegel*, trans. J. Nichols. Ithaca, NY and London: Cornell University Press.

Kramer, L. (2018). *The Hum of the World*. Berkely and London: University of California Press.

Kundera, M. (1984). *The Unbearable Lightness of Being*, trans. H. Heim. New York: Harper.

Kundera, M. (2005). *The Curtain*, trans. L. Asher. London: Faber and Faber, 2007.

Lakoff, G. and Johnson, M. (1980). *Metaphors We Live By*. Chicago, IL and London: Chicago University Press.

Langer, S. (1967). *Mind: An Essay in Human Feeling*. Baltimore, MD: John Hopkins University Press.

Laufer, M. and Laufer, E. (1984). *Adolescence and Developmental Breakdown*. New Haven, CT and London: Yale University Press.

Laufer, E. and Laufer, M. (eds.) (1989). *Developmental Breakdown and Psychoanalytic Treatment in Adolescence*. New Haven, CT and London: Yale University Press.

Leppert, R. (1993). *The Sight of Sound*. Berkeley and London: University of California Press.

Lifton, B. (1994). *Journey of the Adopted Self*. New York: Basic Books.

Lombardi, R. (2008). Time, music and reverie. *J. Amer. Psychoanal Assn*. 56: 1191–1211.

Macarthy, B. (2005). Counterpoints, in *On Incest. Psychoanalytic Perspectives,* ed. G. Ambrosio, pp. 115–120, London and New York: Routledge.

Makari, G. (2008). *Revolution in Mind*. (The creation of psychoanalysis). London: Duckworth.

Malcolm, N. (1986). *Nothing is Hidden*. Oxford: Blackwell.

Mitchell, S. (1991). Contemporary perspectives on self: Toward an integration. *Psychoanal. Dial*. 1: 121–147.

Montaigne, M. de (1580). Solitude, in *The Complete Works*, trans. D. M. Frame. pp. 211–222. London: Everyman Library, 2003.

Murray, L. et al. (1993). Depressed mothers' speech to their infants and its relation to infant gender and cognitive development. *J. Child Psychol. Psychiatry*. 34: 1083–1101.

Nagel, T. (1986). *The View from Nowhere*. New York and Oxford: Oxford University Press.

Nass, M. (1971). Some considerations of a psychoanalytic interpretation of music. *Psychoanal. Q*. 40: 303–316.

Nietzsche, F. (1968). *The Will to Power*, trans. W. Kaufmann and R. J. Hollingdale. New York: Vintage Books.

Ogden, T. (1992a). The dialectically constituted/decentered subject of psychoanalysis. 1. The Freudian subject. *Int. J. Psycho-Anal*. 73: 517–526.

Ogden, T. (1992b). The dialectically constituted/decentered subject of psychoanalysis. 2. The contributions of Winnicott and Klein. *Int. J. Psycho-Anal*. 73: 613–626.

Ogden, T. (1994). *Subjects of Analysis*. London: Karnac.

Parsons, M. (1986). Suddenly finding it really matters: The paradox of the analyst's non-attachment. *Int. J. Psycho-Anal*. 67: 475–488.

Parsons, M. (2006). Ways of transformation, in *Psychoanalysis and Religion in the 21st Century*, ed. David M. Black, pp. 117–131. London and New York: Routledge, New Library of Psychoanalysis.

Parsons, M. (2014). *Living Psychoanalysis*. London: Routledge.

Pontalis, J-B. (1986). *Love of Beginnings*, trans. M-C. Requis and J. Greene. London: Free Associatkon Books, 1993.

Quinodoz, J-M. (1993). *The Taming of Solitude*, trans. P. Slotkin. London and New York: Routledge, New Library of Psychoanalysis.

Quinodoz, J-M. (1996). The sense of solitude in the psychoanalytic encounter. *Int. J. Psychoanal.* 77: 481–496.

Rayner, E. (1991). *The Independent Mind in Psychoanalysis.* London and New York: Free Association Books.

Reik, T. (1953). *The Haunting Melody.* New York: Farrar, Strauss and Young.

Rorty, R. (1989). *Contingency, Irony and Solidarity.* Cambridge: Cambridge University Press.

Rosenfeld, H. (1987). *Impasse and Interpretation.* London: Tavistock Publications and the Institute of Psychoanalysis.

Rousillon, R. (1999). Sexualisation and desexualisation in psychoanalysis, in *Reading French Psychoanalysis*, eds. D. Birksted-Breen, S. Flanders and A. Gibeault, pp. 528–542. London and New York: Routledge.

Said, E. (2006). *On Late Style.* London: Bloomsbury.

Schön, D. (1983). *The Reflective Practitioner.* New York: Basic Books.

Scruton, R. (2014). *The Soul of the World.* Princeton, NJ and Oxford: Princeton University Press.

Searle, J. (1992). *The Rediscovery of the Mind.* Cambridge: MIT Press.

Stern, D. (1985). *The Interpersonal World of the Infant.* New York: Basic Books.

Stern, D. (2010). *Forms of Vitality.* Oxford and New York: Oxford University Press.

Stoller, R. (1976). *Perversion: The Erotic form of Hatred.* London: Harvester.

Stolorow, R. et al. (1994). *The Intersubjective Perspective.* Northvale, NJ: Aronson.

Storr, A. (1988). *Solitude.* London: Andre Deutsch.

Symington, N. (1983). The analyst's act of freedom as agent of therapeutic change. *Int. R. Psycho-Anal.* 10: 283–291.

Tillich, P. (1963). *The Eternal Now.* London: SCM Press.

Viderman, S. (1979). The analytic space: Meaning and problems. *Psychoanal. Q.* 48(2): 257–291.

Weinrib, S. (2012). Is psychoanalysis a matter of subjectivation? *Int. J. Psychoanal.* 93(5): 1115–1135.

Welldon, E. (1998). *Mother, Madonna, Whore.* London and New York: The Guilford Press.

Winnicott, D. (1949). Mind and its relation to the psyche-soma, in *Through Paediatrics to Psychoanalysis: Collected papers*, pp. 243–254. London: Hogarth Press and Institute of Psychoanalysis, 1975.

Winnicott, D. (1958). The capacity to be alone. *Int. J. Psychoanal.* 39: 416–420.

Winnicott, D. (1963). Communicating and not communicating, in *The Maturational Processes and the Facilitating Environment*, London: Hogarth Press, 1965.

Winnicott, D. W. (1969). The use of an object. *Int. J. Psycho-Anal.* 50: 711–716.

Winnicott, D. (1971). *Playing and Reality.* London: Tavistock.

Winnicott, D. (1974). Fear of breakdown. *Int. J. Psychoanal.* 1: 103–107.

Wolf, E. (1988). *Treating the Self.* New York: Guilford Press.

Wolfe, T. (1941). *The Hills Beyond.* New York: Signet Classis, 1968.

Index

For Product Safety Concerns and Information please contact our EU
representative GPSR@taylorandfrancis.com
Taylor & Francis Verlag GmbH, Kaufingerstraße 24, 80331 München, Germany

www.ingramcontent.com/pod-product-compliance
Lightning Source LLC
Chambersburg PA
CBHW050612280326
41932CB00016B/3012

* 9 7 8 1 0 4 1 1 5 4 4 0 2 *